359th Fighter Group

WITHDRAWN
ERAU-PRESCOTT LIBRARY

Aviation Elite Units • 10

OSPREY
PUBLISHING

359th Fighter Group

Jack H Smith

Series editor Tony Holmes

Front cover
15 March 1945 was an historic date for the 359th Fighter Group (FG), for Ray Wetmore scored the only kill made by the entire VIII Fighter Command that day – an Me 163 rocket-powered fighter near Wittenberg. It was also his last aerial victory, taking his overall score to 21.25 kills and one damaged. Wetmore's regular ride, P-51D-10 44-14733 *Daddy's Girl,* **was evidently still undergoing repairs from an incident at the Remagen Bridge because 'Smack' was flying Maj Andy Lemmens' P-51D-15 44-15521** *SCREAMIN' DEMON.* **Of the action itself, he recalled post-mission;**

'South-west of Berlin, I saw two Me 163s circling at about 20,000 ft some 20 miles away, in the vicinity of Wittenberg. I flew over towards them, and while at 25,000 ft started after one a little below me. When I got to within 3000 yards he saw me, turned on his jet and went up in a 70-degree climb. At about 26,000 ft his jet quit and he split-essed. I dove with him and levelled off at 2000 ft at his "six o'clock". During the dive my IAS (Indicated Air Speed) was between 550 and 600 mph. I opened fire at 200 yards. Pieces flew off all over. He made a sharp turn to the right and I gave him another short burst. Roughly half his left wing flew off and he caught fire. The pilot bailed out and I saw the craft crash into the ground.'

Fellow ace 'Pop' Doersch, who flew with many of the 359th's leading pilots during his time in the ETO, said Wetmore was the best. Indeed, he claimed to have 'never seen his equal in battle'. Wetmore had both the flying skill and the 20-15 eyes that make a truly great fighter pilot. He was famous for claiming to be able to tell if an aircraft was an enemy up to 50 miles away (*Cover artwork by Iain Wyllie***)**

First published in Great Britain in 2002 by Osprey Publishing
Elms Court, Chapel Way, Botley, Oxford, OX2 9LP

© 2002 Osprey Publishing Limited

All rights reserved. Apart from any fair dealing for the purpose of private study, research, criticism or review, as permitted under the Copyright, Design and Patents Act 1988, no part of this publication may be reproduced, stored in a retrieval system, or transmitted in any form or by any means, electronic, electrical, chemical, mechanical, optical, photocopying, recording or otherwise without written permission. All enquiries should be addressed to the publisher.

ISBN 1 84176 440 X

Edited by Tony Holmes and Neil Maxwell
Page design by Mark Holt
Cover Artwork by Iain Wyllie
Aircraft Profiles by Tom Tullis
Origination by Grasmere Digital Imaging, Leeds, UK
Printed through Bookbuilders in Hong Kong

00 01 02 03 04   10 9 8 7 6 5 4 3 2 1

ACKNOWLEDGEMENTS
I must thank M/Sgt Bill Wolfinger of the 167th Airlift Wing and Char Baldridge for their assistance in collecting the data that made this book possible. 'Wolfie' also helped to collect data for the aircraft profiles. Special thanks are due to my brother Tom N Smith for his recollections as a B-17 waist gunner in the Eighth Air Force. Walter Given proof-read the text for me, and deserves mention for his work. For a deep look into the soul of the warrior I thank John H Oliphint, a man I respectfully call 'The Predator'. Other members of the group that deserve recognition are David Archibald, Ira J Bisher, Rene Burtner, Anthony Chardella, George A Doersch, Phillip Dupont, Robert Guggemos, Benjamin Hagen, Robert Hatter, Robert Hawkinson, Andrew Lemmens, Larry Lovell, John McAlevey, Charles Mosse, T P Smith, Charles H Staley and Paul E Sundheim.

EDITORS NOTE
To make this new series as authoritative as possible, the Editor would be interested in hearing from any individual who may have relevant photographs, documentation or first-hand experiences relating to the world's elite combat units. Material used will be credited to its original source. Please write to Tony Holmes at 10 Prospect Road, Sevenoaks, Kent, TN13 3UA, Great Britain, or by e-mail at: tony.holmes@osprey-jets.freeserve.co.uk

For details of all Osprey Publishing titles please contact us at:

Osprey Direct UK, P.O. Box 140, Wellingborough, Northants NN8 2FA, UK
E-mail: **info@ospreydirect.co.uk**

Osprey Direct USA c/o MBI Publishing, P.O. Box 1, 729 Prospect Ave, Osceola, WI 54020, USA
E-mail: **info@ospreydirectusa.com**

Or visit our website: **www.ospreypublishing.com**

CONTENTS

INTRODUCTION

More than 75 per cent of the 359th FG's missions were escort, a job closely supervised by Col Avelin P Tacon Jr who did not tolerate a mass exodus from the bomber stream to chase small numbers of enemy fighters. Tacon's strict discipline earned him the nickname 'Hard Tack', and his supervision also won the 359th the undying gratitude of bomber crewmen.

Take the story of Lt David B Archibald, who spotted a crippled B-24 being attacked by a Bf 109. After chasing off the enemy, he moved in close to the bomber and gestured for the pilot to follow him. With two engines out and a third on fire, the crew jettisoned equipment to lighten their aircraft. Flying through an overcast sky at treetop height, Archibald led the Liberator towards an advanced Allied airfield in France. After gaining enough altitude to bail out, and assured they were over friendly territory, the crew jumped. Archibald landed at the airfield, and minutes later met the bomber pilot, who gave him a grateful hug.

The men of the 359th often carried out their assignments with pure abandon, and that spirit was exemplified by Lt Ralph E Kibler Jr when he chased an Fw 190 down the streets of Hamm, Germany, until it crashed head-on into a three-storey building. The 359th's pilots excelled as train-killers and at destroying aircraft on the ground – both very hazardous jobs – and there were missions on which they seemingly tried to machine-gun Germany into submission.

They also lay claim to several firsts and other noteworthy feats. Col Tacon was the first Eighth Air Force pilot to spot and chase the Me 163 rocket fighter, whilst the first Me 163 kill went to Lt Col John B Murphy. On 27 August 1944, Lt Lawrence A Zizka scored the only victory credited to VIII Fighter Command on that day. In a repeat performance, on 15 March 1945, Capt Ray S Wetmore bagged an Me 163 – the odds of the same fighter group scoring the only kill of the day twice are astronomical, especially with hundreds of Allied fighters prowling the skies. See the Significant Missions list for other incidents.

For its actions on 11 September 1944, the 359th received a Distinguished Unit Citation, and for its participation in other major operations six Battle Ribbons to adorn its Guidon. The ribbons are: Air Offensive Europe (preparation for invasion of Normandy); Normandy (invasion support); Northern France (support for the drive across France); Rhineland (support for the airborne invasion of the Netherlands and the drive into the Rhine); Ardennes-Alsace (support during the Battle of the Bulge); and Central Europe (support for the final drive across Germany).

Numbers do not tell the whole story of a combat unit's success, but the 359th's statistics give an indication of what it achieved.

Its operations stretched over 17 months, with 349 missions and 13,455 sorties being flown. The group's losses (including escapees and evaders) stood at 125 pilots and aircraft, with a further 228 fighters being battle-damaged. In return, the 359th destroyed 255.5 enemy aircraft in the air and 121.33 on the ground.

Col Avelin P Tacon Jr, commander of the 359th FG from January 1943 to November 1944. 'Hard Tack' ran a tight ship, and some pilots felt he was preventing them from winning the war, but in truth his discipline kept many of them alive, while those who broke rank often failed to return. Tacon held several command positions during his military career, and retired from the USAF with the rank of major general in 1967

The list goes on – 335 locomotives destroyed, 147 locomotives damaged, 1346 railway cars destroyed or damaged, 144 motor vehicles destroyed, 924,807 rounds of 0.50-cal ammunition expended and 487 500-lb, 325 250-lb and 80 100-lb bombs dropped.

WHAT IS A FIGHTER GROUP?

The 359th FG was assigned to VIII Fighter Command, as a part of the 66th Fighter Wing (FW), until November 1943, when it was moved to the 67th FW. There it would remain, except for a brief return to the 66th during the invasion of Normandy.

Ground support was provided by the 448th Air Service Group (Headquarters Section and Base Services Squadron), the 824th Air Engineering Squadron, the 648th Air Material Squadron and the 3rd Gunnery and Tow-Target Flight. It took about 2000 men to staff the group's combat and support units.

The 359th FG consisted of three squadrons – the 368th, 369th and 370th FSs. Each squadron had 16 fighters, not including spares, divided into four flights. These flights were Red, White, Blue and Yellow. Extra flights were designated as Black and/or Green. These colours were strictly for radio identification, and visual identification was not dealt with until the final months of the war when the dorsal strakes on P-51Ds flown by flight leaders were striped in the appropriate colour. These stripes were either horizontal or vertical.

To visually identify the squadrons, the rudders were painted yellow for the 368th, red for the 369th and dark blue for the 370th. Squadrons were also identified by code letters applied to the sides of the fuselage. These were CV for the 368th, IV for the 369th and CS for the 370th. The double letter codes were applied forward of the national insignia, and the

Lt Ralph E Kibler Jr and the 370th FS's mascot, the ubiquitous 'Flak'. Like so many other talented dogfighters, Kibler fell victim to groundfire while strafing, being shot down and killed in P-51B 42-106865 over Reims-Champagne airfield on 11 May 1944

individual aircraft code letter was located aft. When the number of fighters in a squadron exceeded the number of letters in the alphabet, a duplication occurred. Therefore, in order to distinguish between two fighters with the code letter A, for instance, the A on one of the fighters would either be underlined as A, or similarly capped – that would read as Bar-A.

The letter codes changed only once, and this occurrence was unique to the 359th FG. The switch involved the 370th's code letters some time after the middle of March 1944 when CR changed to CS.

The radio call signs employed by the group were as follows:

Date of Change	359th FG	368th FS	369th FS	370th FS
Used upon arrival in ETO	Wallpaint	Beesnest	Tiretread	Weelass
January 1944	no change	Jackson	no change	Wheeler
17 April 1944	no change	Sonnet	Tinplate	Tailer
23 April 1944	Chairman	Jigger	no change	Redcross
B group call signs	Cavetop	Handy	Earnest	Rollo
C group call sign	Ragtime			

The group's P-47s boasted Olive Drab on uppersurfaces and Neutral Gray undersides. To prevent gunners from mistaking the P-47 for an Fw 190, a 12-in white band was painted on the leading circumference of the engine cowling and chordwise across the vertical and horizontal tail surfaces. This treatment was also given to the P-51 to prevent it from being mistaken for the Bf 109.

The group's distinctive green nose first appeared on the its P-47s during March 1944 in the form of a 24-in medium green band painted around the forward section of the engine cowling. The first green to grace the noses of their Mustangs covered the spinner and the cowling back to the first exhaust stack. In November 1944 the paint changed to dark green, and was extended past the exhaust stacks in a downward curve to the front of the wingroot and wheel wells.

Hours before D-Day, the 359th's P-51s were painted with 'invasion stripes'. One month later these were removed from the uppersurfaces of the wings and fuselage, or sprayed over with a coat of aluminium lacquer.

Both group and squadron insignia featured the unicorn – a symbol of strength and virtue. The 368th FS's motif was a unicorn head with a lightning bolt clenched in its mouth (referred to as a thunderbolt during the P-47 period). The 369th had a unicorn in full stride, superimposed on a lightning bolt, while the 370th's unicorn was displayed in a bucking posture. The group emblem was a left profile of a unicorn head on an escutcheon. Above the head were three stars, with three, five and nine points. Below the escutcheon, in Latin, were the words 'CUM LEONE' (with lions), denoting that the USAAF was fighting alongside the RAF.

The 359th was based at East Wretham (Army Air Force Station 133) in Norfolk, on a former country estate. Wretham Hall was an imposing three-storey structure consisting of some 75 rooms, and was used as living quarters for the officers. The base had previously been occupied by RAF bomber units. Wretham Hall was destroyed by fire in 1949.

THE BEGINNING

The 359th FG was created on 20 December 1942 with the issuing of War Department Order AG 320.2. On 15 January 1943 the First Air Force issued an order activating the group at Westover Field, Massachusetts. Lt Col Avelin P Tacon Jr was put in command.

Throughout March the 359th received enlisted men from various units already stationed at Westover, although most came from training schools. During that month the squadron leaders were assigned – Capt Albert R Tyrrell to the 368th FS, Maj Rockford V Gray to the 369th and Maj John B Murphy to the 370th. Murphy was the only one with combat experience, having flown with the 343rd FG's 11th FS in the Aleutians, where he had shared in the destruction of a Japanese Nakajima E8N 'Dave' floatplane.

Training began in earnest during April, with the 368th and 369th FSs moving to Grenier Field, New Hampshire, while the 370th went to nearby Bedford Army Air Base. Flying time was limited, since each

Two early-build P-47Ds of the 369th FS are seen at Grenier Field, New Hampshire, in April 1943. Incidents in which the landing gear failed to extend on the Thunderbolt were common enough to warrant a mention in the official group records even after the 359th FG had entered combat in the ETO (*Palicka*)

squadron had only two or three P-47s. Between May and July the unit rotated to Republic Field, Long Island, to receive new Thunderbolts, and it was during this time that Lt John H Oliphint looped the Brooklyn Bridge. After landing, he found the airframe was seriously twisted, and officials at the Republic plant were shocked by the damage.

The squadrons gravitated back to Westover Field during August, and at dawn on 2 October 1943 most of the 359th FG left by train for Camp Kilmer, New Jersey. Five days later the group boarded ships in New York Harbor. Headquarters personnel and the 368th boarded the USAT *Argentina*, the 369th the *Thurston* and the 370th took the former Dutch motor vessel *Sloterdyjk*. They were part of a large convoy that sailed before dawn on 8 October.

The *Argentina* docked at Liverpool on 19 October, with the headquarters element and the 368th setting off for East Wretham, in Norfolk. Their trains arrived at Thetford, about five miles south of East Wretham, and the troops marched to their new home. The citizens of Thetford held their noses as they cheered the passing Yanks, Phillip Dupont, a radio technician, stating 'we were quite ripe after all those days on ship without a shower'. Meanwhile, the 369th and 370th disembarked at Glasgow and Gourock.

Lt Col Tacon went to work immediately, but with little emphasis on close order drill or spit and polish. The result was that in less than eight weeks the base was ready for combat operations.

The railway station at Thetford was just five miles south of the group's new base at East Wretham, and the men of the 359th completed the final leg of their long journey from the US on foot

An aerial view of East Wretham prior to the arrival of the 359th FG. The airfield's control tower is obscured by the wingtip visible in the upper right. The hangar right of centre was used by the 370th FS. The strip running parallel to the trailing edge of the wing was the main runway, and it was covered with perforated steel planking during the winter of 1944-45. East Wretham had been hastily brought into service by the RAF in the later summer of 1940, and had been used as a bomber base until occupied by the Eighth Air Force in October 1943

The base control tower at East Wretham was unlike any other at the myriad Eighth Air Force airfields scattered across East Anglia. One thing that was the same, however, was the fleet of crash and recovery vehicles typically clustered alongside the tower, ready to spring into action at a moment's notice

Nearby Wretham Hall, with its 75 rooms, served as home to the 359th's officer corps during the group's time in England. This outstanding stately home was totally destroyed by fire in 1949

VIII Fighter Command required every new fighter group to be led into combat by experienced pilots. To achieve this, the 359th's senior flying officers – Lt Col Tacon and Majs William H Swanson, John Murphy, Albert 'Trigger' Tyrrell and Rockford Gray, as well as 12 captains and lieutenants – were sent on detached service to the 78th FG, at Duxford. Simultaneously, Maj Luther H Richmond of the 352nd FG temporarily moved to East Wretham to act as the 359th's flying group commander.

On 11 December 1943 the 78th FG supported B-24s returning from Emden, in Germany. During the mission the 359th's Capt Chauncey S Irvine and his wingman Lt Col Tacon unsuccessfully bounced a Bf 109, while Lt James R Pino, who was leading a top cover flight, was bounced by German fighters – they too failed to score. That night the detachment returned to East Wretham.

MISSIONS

Due to space limitations, this book cannot cover every mission flown by the 359th, and not all strafing claims have been included.

On the morning of 13 December, 42 P-47s of the 359th had just landed following a practice flight when a field order was received assigning them a fighter sweep over France. Only 36 Thunderbolts were refuelled in time to take part, with Maj Luther Richmond leading the group on its operational debut. The aircraft crossed the enemy coast over Gravelines, made a sweep around St Omer and exited near Le Tréport.

Maj Richmond led again on the 20th as the 359th laid on an escort for B-17s bound for Bremen, in Germany. Of the 59 P-47s that took off, no fewer than 22 returned early – 17 were aborts and five were assigned as their escorts. Eight aborts were due to engine trouble and seven from the failure of drop tanks to release.

R/V (rendezvous) with the bombers was made off Texel Island at 1101 hrs. A flight of P-47s, providing top cover at 32,000 ft, spotted six enemy aircraft at 35,000 ft shadowing the bombers, but did not pursue. Escort was dropped at Zuidlaarder Lake, and the 359th returned on a reciprocal course. Meanwhile, an investigation began into the possible sabotage of the Thunderbolt flown by Lt Herman E King of the 370th FS.

P-47Ds from the 370th FS line up prior to taking off from East Wretham in early 1944. The squadron's CR code changed to CS in mid-March 1944. Wearing the code letters CR-P, P-47D-6 42-74737 was lost on 11 April 1944 when it ran out of fuel after suffering flak damage. Its pilot, Lt Thomas P 'Tepee' Smith, force-landed at Macou, in France, and evaded capture for five months. The aircraft running up to the left of CR-P is P-47D-6 42-74719, which was the first mount of future five-kill ace William Hodges. Indeed, he claimed two Bf 109s destroyed in this P-47 on 10 February 1944, followed by a third Messerschmitt fighter probably destroyed in the same machine on 4 March

A report published in the wake of this mission stated that enemy aircraft had been flying reconnaissance over the bombers, so a 'smack the Hun' order was issued telling fighter groups to 'pursue and destroy'.

Maj Richmond led for the last time on 21 December, the mission being flown in support of Ninth Air Force B-26s bombing *Noball* targets (V1 launch sites) near Calais. Fifty-seven P-47s took off, with a malfunctioning prop causing the only abort. They patrolled for 30 minutes, and a number of pilots saw No 501 Sqn Spitfire IX EP559 explode after it had been mistakenly attacked by an unidentified Thunderbolt. The pilot of the RAF fighter, Flg Off A A Griffiths, bailed out and was made a Prisoner of War (PoW). All the Thunderbolts returned safely except for the aircraft flown by Lt King, who crash-landed on the emergency airfield at Manston, in Kent. He escaped injury, but his P-47 was declared Category E (fit only for salvage of parts). A second investigation into possible sabotage was opened.

Lt Col Tacon led on the 22nd, the group's assignment being a penetration support mission for B-17s and B-24s attacking Osnabrück. The fighters met up with their charges near Zwolle, in the Netherlands, and the escort lasted just 15 minutes before the P-47s' limited range meant they had to head home.

The sabotage mystery then took on a new twist – a saboteur was spotted in the aircraft dispersal area on the 27th and was fired on. He escaped, and damage was discovered to the connections of a drop tank.

Lt Col Tacon was in charge again as the group looked after B-17s raiding Münster on 4 January 1944. They got together east of Dokkum and the escort lasted 12 minutes. The following day the 359th protected B-17s scheduled to bomb ball-bearing plants at Elberfeld. The only event of note occurred near Elsdorf when a B-17 gunner fired on Lt William N Tucker of the 370th and missed. This type of incident happened several times during the following months, and luckily no one was hit.

Sixty-one P-47s of the 359th provided withdrawal support for B-17s and B-24s bombing aircraft factories at Halberstadt and Oschersleben on the 11th. This was the first time the group used 108-gallon drop tanks which replaced the 75-gallon units (after 9 April 1944 the 108-gallon tanks were

Each Thunderbolt in this 368th FS flight was named after a character in Al Capp's popular comic strip *Li'l Abner*. They are, from right to left *MARRYIN' SAM* (assigned to Lt W R Simmons), *PAPPY YOKUM* (P-47D-10 42-75095, assigned to Capt E P Perkins), *DAISY MAE* (P-47D-10 42-75113, assigned to Maj W C Forehand), *MAMMY YOKUM, LI'L ABNER* (assigned to Lt R L Botsford) and *LONESOM' POLECAT* (possibly P-47D-2 42-22468, assigned to Capt R W Hawkinson). This photograph was taken on 28 January 1944

abandoned in favour of 150-gallon tanks). Tacon turned back over the English Channel when his instruments failed, leaving Maj William Swanson to take charge. They made rendezvous close to Amelo, in Belgium, at 1215 hrs, and nine Bf 109s that were spotted in the area were chased off. The 359th then took the lead section of bombers out to Amsterdam and returned to pick up the rest of the force.

At 1232 hrs, 20 miles south of Diepholz, the 368th broke up an attack on the rear box of B-17s by three 'Me 210s' (almost certainly Me 410s). The unit was then bounced by three Bf 109s, one painted blue and the other two light green, with red bands around the fuselage. During the brief engagement that followed, Lt Edward J Hyland was shot down and killed in P-47D 42-8542. The 359th had lost its first pilot in action. A few minutes later Capt James E Buckley, who was leading Yellow Flight of the 370th in P-47D 42-75108, entered a steep dive and disappeared, probably the victim of oxygen equipment failure. More losses occurred upon the group's return to England when two pilots from the 370th were killed in crash landings – Lt William Tucker died at Radnal, Shropshire, and Lt Lynn W Hair was killed at Chipping Warden, in Northamptonshire, when his P-47 hit a tree and exploded.

Following the carnage of 11 January, the 359th enjoyed a red-letter day on 29 January, with Lt John Oliphint (dubbed 'The Mad Rebel') scoring the group's first kill. Tacon, now a full colonel, was leading a withdrawal support mission for B-17s and B-24s returning from Frankfurt when, at 1215 hrs near Malmédy, in Belgium, Lt Emer H Cater of the 368th's Red Flight spotted a glossy, light green Bf 110 5000 ft below him. Diving from 27,000 ft, Oliphint (of the 369th) succeeded in getting onto the tail of the Bf 110 ahead of his group mates, and ignoring the rear gunner's defensive fire, hit the fighter with a well-aimed burst. He recalls;

Armourers from the 369th FS have just finished hanging this 500-lb general purpose bomb beneath an unidentified P-47. This photograph was probably taken on 28 January 1944 – the group flew its only bombing mission prior to Valentine's Day on this date (*Chardella*)

Lt John Houston Oliphint (above) and Maj Rockford Vance Gray (below right) both participated in the action that led to the group's first aerial kill, on 29 January 1944. 'Ollie' and 'Rocky' were jointly credited with destroying a Bf 110, although in reality the latter pilot only achieved a few hits on the already doomed German fighter. Oliphint later saw action both in Korea and Vietnam, before retiring from the USAF with the rank of major. Gray was the first commander of the 369th FS, and he later transferred to the Ninth Air Force in early March 1944. Gray scored 6.5 victories before being killed in a flying accident on 4 September 1944 whilst at the controls of a 371st FG P-47D. This early shot of Rockford Gray reveals a 369th FS badge adorning the fuselage of his unidentified Thunderbolt

'Pieces of the aeroplane flew all over the sky in front of me. Tightening up my turn and easing over toward his right engine, I fired another quick burst and the engine blew apart. The engine then broke away and peeled back toward me so that I had to pull up to dodge it. That gave "Rocky" Gray, who had closed in behind me, a chance to get a quick shot at my condemned enemy aircraft.'

'Ollie' moved alongside the Bf 110 and saw that the gunner had lost his right arm and part of his head. Lt Cater and Capt Clifton Shaw chased the spiralling aircraft and scored a few hits on the fighter's port engine, which began trailing smoke. 'Ollie' then hammered the Bf 110 again, and the pilot bailed out. Low on fuel, he put his P-47 into an economical cruise and escorted a crippled B-17 back to England. Later, when Crew Chief Earl 'Big Red' Wallace serviced Oliphint's engine, he found a finger belonging to the Bf 110's gunner. Ollie buried it amongst the ruins of nearby St Andrew's, a Norman church.

The following day Col Tacon led a withdrawal support mission for B-17s and B-24s returning from Brunswick and Hannover. They crossed the coast at Ijmuiden, in the Netherlands, and made R/V near Herzlake. The 369th attacked eight Ju 88s flying line abreast, which were preparing to attack the bombers near Haselünne. Lt Robert L Thacker downed one and claimed a probable, while Lts Robert L Pherson and Luster H Prewitt damaged two more. Minutes later six Bf 109s were engaged, and Maj Rockford Gray and Lt Robert J Booth each claimed a fighter apiece, while Capt Niven K Cranfill damaged a third Messerschmitt near Lingen. Gray's P-47 was found to have parts of the pilot he had killed stuck to it.

During this period the 359th managed to put up more aircraft than any other fighter group in the Eighth Air Force, and its pilots showed a remarkable ability to fly on instruments in extremely poor weather.

Line shacks built from shipping crates offered shelter for mechanics forced to work in the open. This personalised hut (adorned with pilots' names, and their scores) belonged to the 369th FS's 'D' Flight

One of the first pilots posted to the 369th FS upon its formation in early 1943, Lt Cecil William 'Bird Dog' Crawford vanished while returning from the mission of 3 February 1944. Flying P-47D-4 42-22791, he was the squadron's first combat loss

On 3 February the group escorted B-17s bombing targets around Emden and Wilhelmshaven, with R/V being made over Meppel, in the Netherlands. Lt Lester G Taylor of the 369th aborted and headed home, with Lt Robert C Thomson as escort. Thirty miles from the Dutch coast they encountered two Fw 190s, and Thomson made a head-on attack against one, scoring a kill. The other fighter fled. Over Emden, three P-47s of the 369th's White Flight were damaged by flak, leaving its fourth member, Lt Cecil W 'Bird Dog' Crawford, to head for another flight some distance in front of him . He failed to make it, last being seen heading west near Texel Island in P-47D 42-2279.

Upon returning to England, Lt Charles W Hipsher of the 370th ran low on fuel and made a wheels-up landing at Oulton, in Norfolk, striking several objects on the runway which was then still under construction. Lt Thomson landed his battle-damaged 'Jug' on the emergency airfield at Woodbridge.

On 8 February the 359th provided penetration support for B-24s bombing *Noball* targets at Siracourt, in France. For the pilots, it was a boring run.

However, a penetration support mission for B-17s raiding industrial targets at Brunswick on the 10th proved to be a different story. Nine P-47s returned early, including five that failed to find the rest of the group because of cloud formations reaching up to 20,000 ft. R/V was made near Egmond, in the Netherlands, and the force crossed in at 1039 hrs. At 1110 hrs, near the Dutch town of Gramsbergen, the 369th and 370th were bounced by between 15 and 20 Bf 109s. During the fight the 359th FG claimed seven fighters destroyed and an eighth damaged. Amongst the successful pilots were future 370th FS aces Lts William Hodges (who was credited with two kills) and Ray Wetmore.

And whilst the 369th and 370th FS fended off the enemy fighters, the 368th maintained escort until reaching Bawinkel, in Germany. The mission was deemed to be such a success that the 359th received a letter of commendation from Lt Gen Carl Spaatz, commanding general of US Strategic Air Forces in Europe.

20 February 1944 was the first day of 'Big Week', which saw the Eighth Air Force launch an all-out assault on German aircraft production facilities and airfields. As part of this operation, B-17s bombed an airfield at Leipzig, with the 359th providing penetration escort. Making a successful combat debut on this mission was an anti-jamming device built into the group's radios by Capt Alfred M Swiren, the 359th's Communications Officer.

Maj William Swanson led the group on an uneventful penetration escort for B-17s raiding Brunswick on the 21st, and Col Tacon was back in the lead on the 22nd, as the 359th provided penetration escort for B-17s bombing several German cities. The force entered Germany near Valkenberg, in Belgium, at 1215 hrs, and 45 minutes later near Hamm, in Germany, future ace Lt George A Doersch of the 370th saw a B-17 explode off to his left. He and Tacon flew over to investigate and encountered a solitary 'Fw 190D', which Doersch destroyed. At 1305 hrs the 370th was jumped by ten-plus Bf 109s, and future ace Maj John Murphy bagged one and Lt Albert T Niccolai damaged another. The 368th joined in the action at 1312 hrs when three Bf 109s were seen attacking an aborting B-17. All three were destroyed, with kills going to Capt Charles E 'Carlos' Mosse, and Lts Andrew T Lemmens and Cater.

On 25 February Col Tacon introduced a policy of giving squadron commanders experience at both briefing and leading the group, resulting in Maj Swanson of the 369th heading the 359th as it provided penetration escort for B-17s raiding Regensburg.

In the days following this mission heavy snow fell in East Anglia, and it was not until the weather abated on 4 March that groundcrews were able to thaw the P-47s' control surfaces.

Maj John Murphy then led a penetration escort for B-17s in a raid on Berlin. Near Bonn, the 370th's Lt Wetmore spotted about 75 enemy fighters 'nine o'clock high' to the bombers, and Blue and White Flights turned into the approaching bandits, breaking up their attack.

The following claims were subsequently made by the 370th – Lt Wetmore was credited with one Bf 109 destroyed and one damaged, Lt William R Hodges one Bf 109 probable, Lt Harold D 'Holly' Hollis and Capt Charles Mosse one Bf 109 damaged apiece, and Maj John Murphy one Bf 109 shared destroyed with Lts Alan C Porter and Paul Bateman, as well as an 'Fw 190D' shared destroyed with Bateman. The group then penetrated to Neuenkirchen, before withdrawing to Malmédy and setting up an area patrol. Meanwhile, Blue and Yellow Flights of the 369th ran into between 40 and 50 Bf 109s near Cologne, and in a running defensive battle Lt Richard H Broach claimed a Messerschmitt as a probable.

There were two missions flown on 6 March, with the first being a penetration escort for B-17s bound for Berlin. Maj Murphy led after

Lt Charles H Kruger of the 369th scored one of his two aerial kills on 15 March 1944. Serving with the 359th FG from June 1943 to August 1944, Kruger completed 89 missions totalling 300.30 hours of combat flying. All three of his assigned fighters were christened *Nancy June*

Future ranking 359th FG ace Lt Ray Wetmore scored two Bf 109 kills on 16 March 1944 in this particular P-47D-10 (42-75068). The fighter features eight crosses below the cockpit, denoting that this photograph was taken after 22 April, when Wetmore claimed his fourth full aerial victory. The remaining markings signify a quarter of a kill, one damaged and two ground strafing victories. This P-47 was code CS-R when he claimed his Bf 109s on 16 March (*DeGraves*)

Col Tacon aborted with radio trouble. The second mission was a withdrawal escort for the returning B-17s, and Maj Clifton Shaw led after Tacon was yet again hampered by radio problems. On the latter operation, the 368th and 369th engaged enemy fighters attacking B-17s and B-24s near Vechta. The 368th's Capt Wayne N Bolefahr claimed a Bf 109 destroyed, whilst Lt Cater damaged a Fw 190 and Lt Raymond B Janney III probably destroyed a second Bf 109. In the same action, the 369th's Lt Robert L Pherson was also credited with a Bf 109 destroyed, the fighter diving away with its engine smoking and cockpit on fire. Squadronmate Lt Robert Booth forced the pilot of an Fw 190 to bail out, although the German plunged to his death when his parachute canopy split upon deployment.

The 359th was given the job of keeping an eye on B-24s bombing Brunswick on 15 March. They all met up at 1150 hrs over Hannover, and 20 minutes later, near Steinhurder Lake, about a dozen Bf 109s approached the 368th in close formation. Two flights broke into the bandits, and Lt Thomas J McGeever destroyed one and damaged two more. At 1215 hrs Yellow and Green Flights of the 369th engaged between six and ten Bf 109s, and Lt Charles H Kruger claimed both a kill and a probable. Low on fuel, he and Lts Frank S Fong and Robert Thacker hit the deck and headed for home. As they crossed the Netherlands they saw between 25 and 30 Bf 109s flying a parallel course over the Zuider Zee. The Thunderbolt pilots hugged the terrain and escaped detection, snagging trees and powerlines in the process.

Maj Albert Tyrrell led the first mission of 16 March – a penetration escort for B-17s bombing Augsburg in Germany. The group made R/V

Capt John B Hunter of the 368th poses with his younger brother Robert, who served as an armourer in the same squadron. John, who flew with the 368th from April 1943 through to April 1945, scored three kills (one in the air and two on the ground)

near Compiègne, in France, and at 1025 hrs near St Dizier the bombers were attacked by four Bf 109s diving from 30,000 ft. The 368th and 369th broke up the attack, and Lt Howard A Linderer of the 369th flamed one of the bandits.

Escort was dropped during the engagement, and on the way out at Sommesous Lt Wetmore, leading Blue Flight of the 370th, spotted 25 bandits diving on a formation of B-17s. As the Germans passed through the 'Forts', Wetmore led a diving attack on two Fw 190s. Firing a long burst into one as he entered compressibility, Wetmore was shocked to see the enemy fighter explode. As the P-47s climbed back up to the bombers, two more Fw 190s appeared, and Wetmore claimed his second Fw 190 kill of the mission.

Attempting to reach the bombers for a second time, the flight had to dodge two parachutes from a B-17 which was under attack by an Fw 190. As Blue Flight turned towards the bandit, he broke off the attack and headed for the deck. The withdrawal support mission for the Augsburg raiders was carried off uneventfully.

On 19 March the 359th provided area support for B-17s raiding *Noball* targets around Lens, in France. During the course of the mission Lt Joseph M Ashenmacher of the 368th was hit in the left hand by a piece of flak, and upon returning to base his left index finger had to amputated. This would duly earned him the group's first Purple Heart.

26 March saw another *Noball* support mission flown over the Pas de Calais. Meanwhile, back at East Wretham the group took delivery of its first six P-51Bs (two for each squadron), and pilots prepared for their transition to the type.

Lt Andrew T Lemmens scored the first of his three aerial kills on 22 February 1944. Serving with the 368th from June 1943 through to May 1944, and then the 370th up until to April 1945, he flew 133 missions totalling 524.55 hours in combat. Lemmens ended the war with the 359th FG's HQ Flight

Lt Frank S Fong, the only Chinese-American pilot in the ETO at that time, shot down an Fw 190 on 27 March 1944 whilst serving with the 369th FS

That same day a B-17 from the 452nd BG provided a most pleasant surprise when it buzzed the base and dropped a bottle attached to a parachute made from a handkerchief. In it was the following message;

'To The P-47 Boys,

To you who fly and keep them flying. Many thanks for the wonderful work you are doing for us who are up here in the big ones. You are to all of us a million-dollar sight when you help us on every mission. Again, we the boys of this Fort *SUNRISE SERENADE* want to thank each and every one of you for your protection to us as we make each mission.

Thanks a million.

Signed, the crew of the *SUNRISE SERENADE*'

'BILL'S BUZZ BOYS'

The unit known as 'Bill's Buzz Boys' was formed by Col Glenn E Duncan, commander of the 353rd FG, with the approval of Maj Gen William E Kepner, Commanding General VIII Fighter Command. Their goal was to find the best methods for attacking ground targets, especially airfields. They literally 'wrote the book'.

Sixteen volunteers, four each from the 353rd, 355th, 359th and 361st FGs, reported to Col Duncan on 15 March 1944. The 359th's pilots were from the 369th FS, and their leader was Capt Charles C 'Chief' Ettlesen, considered one of the 359th's best pilots. His fellow volunteers were Lts John Oliphint, Clifford E Carter and Robert L Thacker. The unit was named 'Bill's Buzz Boys' as a mark of respect for Gen Bill Kepner.

On 26 March Col Duncan led 12 Thunderbolts of the so-called 353rd 'C' FG on its first mission. Blue Flight, comprising the 359th's pilots, attacked the airfield at Châteaudun, in France. Capt Ettlesen led, and as they approached the target at 425 mph, he strafed a hangar but hit a power pole that cut half way through his P-47's wing before snapping. Oliphint had destroyed a twin-engined aircraft and damaged three hangars by the time his P-47 took a 20 mm shell in the main fuel tank, which miraculously failed to explode. Carter damaged an He 111 and one blister hangar.

On the 29th Ettlesen led Blue Flight as they attacked the airfield at Quakenbrück, setting a hangar on fire and damaging a barracks. He then destroyed a locomotive and shared in the destruction of four others. Oliphint also strafed two passenger trains, damaging the locomotives and 19 coaches. He then attacked a freight train, destroying the locomotive and damaging several wagons, two coal trains, destroying the locomotives and derailing several wagons and damaged a barge, killing five German soldiers. Thacker damaged a barracks and a railway station as well as sharing in the damage inflicted on the locomotives. Carter destroyed two Me 410s on the airfield, and as he pulled up he riddled an administration building with 0.50-cal shells. He later shared in the strafing of five locomotives.

Ettlesen led 'The Boys' on 1 April as they sought out airfields in northwest Germany. His White Flight failed to find its assigned target due to poor visibility, so they pressed on to Böhmte, where they found eight stationary locomotives in a marshalling yard. As Ettlesen stated in his report, they 'shot the hell out of them'. On the way out, passing over the eastern edge of the Zuider Zee, Ettlesen was bounced by two Bf 109s out of

On 19 March 1944 Lt Joseph Ashenmacher of the 368th was wounded in the hand by flak near Lens during a *Noball* escort mission. Upon returning to base he had to have his left index finger amputated. This wound earned him the dubious honour of receiving the 359th's first Purple Heart. Despite his misfortune, Ashenmacher went on to complete his tour in October 1944

Maj Gen William E Kepner, the 'Bill' in 'Bill's Buzz Boys'. Lt Col Grady L 'Snuffy' Smith, the 359th's group 'exec', stands behind Kepner

Lt John H Oliphint (left), Lt Robert Leroy Thacker (middle) and Capt Charles Campbell Ettlesen (right) recreate a briefing for the press in late March 1944. The cardinal rules for attacking ground targets, formulated by 'Bill's Buzz Boys', were come in fast, come in low and make only one pass. Of these three highly skilled strafers, only Thacker would not fall victim to the deadly German flak

the sun. Carter answered his call for help and hit one of the attackers, the Thunderbolt pilot later confirming that the Bf 109 was trailing black smoke when he lost it in cloud cover. He was credited with a probable.

On the 8th Ettlesen was in charge as they headed to the same area of Germany, White Flight strafing targets of opportunity around Dummer Lake. After attacking a motor launch, Oliphint noticed that Clifford Carter was missing, and he circled around Böhmte looking for him. He saw that the side of a two-storey house had been damaged, but there was no aircraft debris around. It was assumed that Carter had been hit by flak, struck the house (in P-47D 42-22464) and carried on before sending a radio transmission stating that he was bailing out. Initially listed as missing in action, Carter's death was later confirmed. As they headed back to England, Ettlesen and Thacker escorted a B-24 straggler to the coast.

It was probably on this mission that Lt Oliphint scored an unconfirmed kill. Returning alone, with only 50 rounds of ammunition left per gun, he met an 'Fw 190D' head-on. Like two ancient knights in a jousting tournament, they tore each other's aircraft apart, the Focke-Wulf sustaining hits in the engine and radiator, and having one cowl gun blown out of its mounts. Oliphint's Thunderbolt had two cylinders shot off the engine, the right flap torn away and the gun camera destroyed. There was a hole in the right wing where the wheel had been, and his hydraulics were useless. 'Ollie' made a dead-stick landing at Manston, where astounded groundcrews counted 423 holes in his P-47. He personally had not suffered a scratch in the encounter, but the film that would have given him a confirmed kill was gone.

Lt John F Starr of the 350th FS/353rd FG led on the 12th, which proved to be the final mission for 'The Buzz Boys'. Oliphint made the only claim for Blue Flight when he destroyed a locomotive and set two wagons on fire. The unit was disbanded that evening, and the 359th's pilots returned to East Wretham the following day.

Whilst the strafers had been away with the 353rd, the remaining 359th FG pilots had continued to venture to France on escort missions. One such operation occurred on 27 March, when Col Tacon led the escort for B-17s bombing airfields at Chartres, Tours and La Rochelle. At 1410 hrs, near Châteaudun, the 368th had a brief and scoreless skirmish with Bf 109s. At the same time, near Chartres, the 370th had just made R/V at 15,000 ft when 15+ bandits were spotted at 10,000 ft heading for the bombers. As Capt Daniel D McKee led Red Flight in a diving attack, Lt Howard E Grimes aborted with a malfunctioning prop. McKee claimed an Fw 190 as a probable, and was hammering away at a Bf 109 when a second Messerschmitt latched on to his tail and inflicted minor damage. McKee shook off his attacker, and as the three remaining P-47s formed up to return to base, they were jumped by five Bf 109s. Lt John E Kerns (in P-47D 42-7891) was last seen being pursued by three of the fighters, and he was later listed as killed in action.

A stern-faced Col Tacon poses for the camera prior to climbing aboard his P-47D-5 (42-8637) in early 1944. He is dressed in typical flying gear for a frontline Eighth Air Force fighter pilot in the ETO at this stage of the war, namely bib overalls, tucked into RAF 1940 Pattern boots, an A-2 leather jacket and a B-3 life preserver. His Type C helmet is also of British origin, as these were renowned for not only giving better ear protection than their American equivalent, but also improved radio clarity due both to its deeper ear cups and better sealing around the ears themselves. Attached to the helmet is a US issue A-14 mask, B-7 goggles and R/T lead. Finally, Tacon is weighed down with a B-5 seat parachute harness

McKee and the other survivor from Red Flight shook off their adversaries and headed for England. Lt Charles V Cunningham's P-47 also suffered major damage from a bandit that bounced him from out of the sun, the wing spar being severed, a cylinder shot off the engine and a tyre blown out. Despite this ravaging, Cunningham flew 190 miles and made a safe landing at Shoreham airfield on the Sussex coast. Finally, at 1430 hrs the 369th engaged enemy fighters near Gallardon, in France and Lt Frank Fong (the only Chinese-American pilot in the ETO at that time) bagged an Fw 190, while Lt Robert Pherson downed a Bf 109.

Poor weather blighted the 359th's mission on 9 April when, after several delays, Col Tacon led the group on a withdrawal support operation for B-24s bombing Tutow, in Germany. They crossed in south of De Kooi, in the Netherlands, and went on to Hannover, where the weather was so bad that no bombers could be found to escort.

On the 11th the 359th, led by Maj Chauncey Irvine, looked after B-17s bombing aircraft factories at Sorau. Once the bombers were clear of the target area, the P-47 pilots strafed targets as they headed home. Further support for the bombers was provided from Holdorf to Fallersleben, where Red Flight of the 370th FS bounced seven bandits attacking the Flying Fortresses.

Lt Robert W 'Hawk' Hawkinson of the 368th and his Thunderbolt *LONESOM' POLECAT* (possibly P-47D-2 42-22468) in late January 1944. One of the unit's original pilots, Hawkinson's tour came to an abrupt end on 2 August 1944 when his Mustang (P-51D-5 44-13386) was hit by flak over Rouen. Bailing out, he suffered a broken ankle on landing and was hidden by French civilians until the area was liberated by the Allies in late August. Hawkinson had flown some 81 missions totalling 332 combat hours prior to being shot down

On 11 April 1944 Lt Will D Burgsteiner of the 370th FS destroyed four Fw 190s and damaged a fifth during a strafing attack on Gütersloh airfield. These proved to be the only victories he would score during his combat tour, which ended in December 1944

Lt Thomas P 'Tepee' Smith and 'Flak' stand in front of the former's P-47D-6 42-74737 just days prior to him being shot down in this very machine on 11 April 1944

Lt George A 'Pop' Doersch downed an Fw 190 after a long chase at an altitude of just 50 ft, and Lt Ralph E Kibler damaged a Bf 109. As Lt Elmer N Dunlap tried to climb back up to altitude with Red Flight, he experienced a problem with the throttle of his P-47D (42-75079), and while separated was bounced by five bandits. He 'bagged' one Fw 190 and damaged another before his engine was hit by a 20 mm shell fired from a Bf 109. As Dunlap headed for home, his engine quit west of the German town of Lingen, and the P-47 crashed into trees. The American was unconscious when he was extricated from the wreck and taken prisoner.

When the escort ended at Fallersleben, the 370th went hunting for ground targets. Whilst passing over Gütersloh with two crippled bombers, Yellow Flight spotted an airfield and dropped down to strafe it. In the next few minutes Lt Will D Burgsteiner destroyed four Fw 190s and damaged another, and Capt Samuel R Smith claimed two Focke-Wulf fighters destroyed on the ground and a third shot down over the airfield – although the latter was seen to cartwheel on impact, Smith was only awarded a probable kill. Lt Robert M Callahan also damaged five Fw 190s.

As this was going on, Blue and White Flights strafed an airfield near Volkenrod, and their claims included four Ju 88s destroyed and five damaged. Lt Thomas P 'Tepee' Smith, who was separated from his squadron, made a single pass on an Fw 190 taking off at Hamm and was hit

Proof that the Thunderbolt could 'take a licking and keep on ticking'. A groundcrewman points out the exit hole for a 20 mm shell that struck this 369th P-47 over Germany. It is unlikely that the pilot would have survived such devastation had the shell struck the fighter four feet further forward (*Ethell*)

Crew Chief Sgt George M Rinaldi poses with his flak-damaged P-47, this time from the 368th FS

by flak (in P-47D 42-74737). He ran out of fuel and crash-landed at Macou, in France. While putting down, 'Tepee' accidentally fired his guns, scattering a German bicycle patrol ahead of him. Running into trees bordering a hay field to discard his flight helmet, he then sneaked back into the field. The Germans failed to find him, and the following day he was taken in by the Lefebvre family across the Franco-Belgian border in Quevaucamps. After five months in hiding in Belgium, the local Resistance arranged for Smith to be smuggled into Switzerland, but when he got into the car that was to take him, he discovered too late that the other 'passengers' were Germans, and he ended up in St Gilles Prison in Brussels.

Smith was loaded into a railway wagon with other PoWs, bound for Germany, but during the night the train was derailed and the prisoners escaped. Fortunately, 'Tepee' came across British Army units and rejoined the 359th on 16 September 1944.

On the same mission that saw the demise of 'Tepee' Smith, Lt James Pino of the 368th was lost on his way out over the Netherlands when his engine lost oil pressure and seized. He belly-landed P-47D 42-75141, hitting an outhouse and burrowing into a haystack, before being captured.

Maj Niven Cranfill led the group on a dedicated strafing mission to Oldenburg, in Germany, on 15 April, the 369th providing top cover while the 368th and 370th dealt out the destruction. The 368th was assigned one airfield for each of its four flights, but they proved to be devoid of aircraft, so targets of opportunity were hit instead. Near Aurich, Blue and White Flights claimed one locomotive destroyed, as well as damaging three radar installations, two flak towers and two barracks.

Red Flight of the 370th strafed an airfield near Oldenburg, where Lts Robert Callahan and Harold Hollis each destroyed a Ju 88, and Capt Daniel McKee damaged both an aircraft resembling a P-47 and a biplane, as well as one flak position. Blue Flight strafed an airfield at Kayhauserfeld, where Lt Samuel J Huskins damaged a flak tower and Lt George Doersch almost collided with a Ju 88 approaching the field. Separated from his flight while dodging flak, he spotted the Ju 88 again, near Varel. After being fired, on the German lowered his wheels and took refuge over an army camp. During numerous passes the rear gunner was evidently killed but the severely damaged bomber remained airworthy. Eventually the flak became so intense that 'Pop' headed home.

On the 19th Maj Albert R Tyrrell led a penetration escort mission for B-24s raiding airfields at Paderborn and Gütersloh. Only 32 P-47s flew this mission, which was ten less than usual. The reduced number was caused by a spate of engine oil pressure failures, resulting in an abnormally high number of engine changes. After the escort was dropped, the 369th strafed German targets between Osnabrück and Minden.

Three days later Capt McKee led the 359th on penetration and target support for B-17s raiding the marshalling yards at Hamm. Once over the target, Yellow Flight of the 370th spotted about 20 bandits at 'nine o'clock' to the bombers. With Red Flight as cover, Yellow Flight broke into the enemy. All but one of their German foes turned to meet the P-47s, and the lone attacker was shot down by a B-17 gunner. During the

Initially plagued with gremlins, the big Pratt & Whitney R-2800 would duly prove both reliable and capable of running with entire cylinders shot away. Conducting a routine service on the line, these groundcrewmen are (from top left to lower right) T/Sgt Jack Linder, S/Sgt Earl Sneddon, Sgt Carrol Erickson and Sgt Chester Sawyer. As this photograph clearly shows, the P-47 was a big aircraft

Capt Howard L Fogg Jr of the 368th FS applies the finishing touches to an oil painting based on his recent combat experiences. He is using a little artistic license here, for Fogg never actually shot anything down during his 76-mission (271 combat hours) tour, which lasted from May 1943 to May 1944 with the 368th FS, and June to September 1944 with the 370th FS. Fogg was later renowned among railway buffs for his paintings of trains

encounter Lt Ralph Kibler claimed two Fw 190s destroyed, with one of the pilots bailing out, Lt Harold Hollis claimed one 'Fw 190D' destroyed and Lt Raymond B Lancaster was also credited with a Focke-Wulf kill, the pilot bailing out – he also claimed to have damaged a second Fw 190.

On the debit side, the 370th's Lt Earl W Thomas Jr was shot down (in P-47D 42-75262) and killed on his first combat mission.

The 369th also got a piece of the action that day, with Lts Harry L 'Matt' Matthew and Robert J 'Posty' Booth each bagging an Fw 190. Matthew's kill was notable because he caught the German hugging the ground and dragging a section of wire fence on his tailwheel!

On the way out, about 40 miles north of Hamm, the 370th's Blue Flight strafed a marshalling yard, and while looking for someone to join up with, Lt Ray Wetmore slid his elderly P-47C (41-6282) in alongside the Fw 190 flown by Leutnant Herbert Konrad Eh. The German pilot realised too late what had happened, and failed to escape before Wetmore blasted his Fw 190. Eh pulled up to 1500 ft and bailed out.

The first of two missions flown on 27 April saw the 359th given the task of protecting B-17s and B-24s that were once again bombing *Noball* targets around the Pas de Calais. Three 'Forts' were seen going down as a result of flak, with only ten 'chutes spotted. The boring job of providing support for *Noball* missions was not made any easier when one group of bombers was seen making no fewer than seven runs over a wooded area, apparently without dropping their loads. The second mission was a withdrawal support operation for B-17s attacking an airfield at Nancy, in France. Escort was dropped north of Brussels, but a section of P-47s led by Capt

Premier 359th FG ace Lt Robert J 'Posty' Booth scored at least one of his four Thunderbolt kills in P-47D-5 42-8695 *Oily Boid*, downing a Bf 109 on 25 April 1944 (*Hess*)

P-47D-22 42-26060 was one of the very few natural metal finish Thunderbolts received by the 359th in the early spring of 1944. It is believed that none of these machines saw any actual combat before being passed on to the Ninth Air Force (*Lovell*)

McKee followed the 'Forts' back to England. This prevented German night intruders from slipping into the bomber formations and turning a landing pattern into a shooting gallery. Just such an attack had occurred five days earlier, resulting in the loss of 13 B-24s and one B-17.

On 29 April the 359th escorted B-17s bombing Berlin. R/V was made near Egmond, in the Netherlands, and the 'Forts' were taken to Hannover, where a large force of enemy fighters approached them. The 370th broke up the attack, and Lt Charles Cunningham destroyed an Fw 190. Having dropped the escort, Red and Yellow Flights of the 370th were orbiting an airfield near the German city when they were bounced by 15+ Bf 109s. After a brief encounter in which there were no claims or losses, the flights strafed a nearby marshalling yard, after which Lt Charles W Hipsher claimed seven of 14 locomotives destroyed.

Capt McKee nursed his P-47 back to England with a windscreen obscured by oil leaking from a cylinder that had blown over Germany. Soon after crossing the Suffolk coast his fighter caught fire and he was forced to make an emergency landing at the 390th BG's base at Framlingham. The Thunderbolt nosed over soon after hitting the ground, flipping onto its back. McKee, however, crawled out of the twisted remains in good shape.

At the end of April the 359th had about 140 fighters on hand, 76 of which were Mustangs. The following month would see most of the group's P-47D-22s passed on to the Ninth Air Force following its total re-equipment with the new North American fighter.

On 3 May pilots from all three squadrons within the 359th FG attended a lecture on flying the Mustang given by Lt Col John C Meyer of the 352nd FG (see *Osprey Aviation Elite 8 - 352nd Fighter Group* for further details). The rest of the day was devoted to transitional flying. Missions dominated by limited range and running defensive combat were now at an end.

On the 6th Lt Col Swanson led the first all-Mustang mission as the group provided cover for B-24s hitting *Noball* targets. The 359th had by now come to hate these uneventful *Noball* missions.

Two days later the 359th escorted B-24s bound for Brunswick, in Germany. The bombers were attacked by between 50 and 75 Bf 109s south-east of Bremen, and in the ensuing mêlée, the 359th claimed 12 destroyed, one probable and three damaged. With four P-47 kills already to his credit, Lt Robert 'Posty' Booth (in P-51B 43-7199) of the 369th got two Bf 109s and an Fw 190 to claim the group's first triple kill – and become the 359th's premier ace to boot!

Close behind him was Lt Doersch of the 370th who, having already downed one Fw 190 and damaged a second earlier in the engagement, destroyed a Bf 109 with just one operable gun. With his ammunition exhausted, Doersch pressed home his dummy attacks so successfully that he forced the German pilot to jettison his canopy and bail out. Doersch's score now stood at four destroyed and two damaged.

Despite this success, the 359th lost two pilots. Lt Stanley E Sackett of the 369th became separated from his flight during the engagement, and his body was found in the wreckage of his P-51B (42-106904) north-east of Neustadt. A similar discovery was made by enemy troops in a forest near Celle, in Germany, Lt Alan C Porter of the 370th having crashed to his death in P-51B (43-7179).

In a worrying postscript to this mission, 369th FS CO Maj Chauncey Irvine filed a complaint that his unit had been jumped by P-38s from the the 20th FG.

Col Tacon led the group on the 11th as it provided target and

A pair of 368th FS Thunderbolts head out on 4 May 1944 on the Republic fighter's last mission with the 359th FG. That day saw the 359th put up a 'mixed bag' of P-47s and P-51s on a penetration support mission for B-17s attacking targets of opportunity around Brunswick, in Germany. Note that both fighters feature oversized national insignia on the undersides of both wings

Lt Robert John 'Posty' Booth (left) of the 369th FS poses with Lt George 'Pop' Doersch of the 370th. On 8 May 1944 20-year-old Booth scored the group's first triple kill to 'make ace', while Doersch claimed two to boost his score to four victories – he became an ace exactly three weeks later. Post-war, when asked his opinion of the Mustang, Booth said it was his favourite fighter, and the only time he wished he hadn't been in one was the day (8 June) flak brought him down (*Chardella*)

withdrawal escort for B-24s bombing the marshalling yards at Mulhouse, in France. A preliminary sweep was followed by an early R/V over Besancon at 1507 hrs. The results of the bombing were noted to be good, and no enemy aircraft were encountered. The escort finished near Epinal at 1537 hrs and the 370th dropped down to strafe. At 1620 hrs they attacked an airfield at Reims-Champagne, where Lt Harold Hollis destroyed an Me 410. Lt 'Smack' Wetmore damaged two flak towers and two gun emplacements, while Capt McKee strafed hangars. Meanwhile, the German gunners were getting their range.

As Lt William Hodges made a pass, the hydraulic system of his P-51B (43-24833) was struck. Heading away from the airfield, he had not travelled far when the propeller locked up, forcing him to bail out near Peronne. A future five-kill ace, Hodges evaded capture and finally made it back to England in September.

Red Flight was last across the field, by which time the flak gunners were waiting for them. The first Mustang downed was 42-106865, flown by Lt Ralph Kibler. With three aerial victories already to his credit, and undoubtedly a future ace had he survived, Kibler perished when his fighter hit the ground at high speed. Lt Edward J Maslow was more fortunate, as he managed to gain a little height in his gravely damaged Mustang (P-51C 42-103343) before bailing out and into captivity. Lt Doersch's P-51 was also hit by an explosive 20 mm round, draining its right wing fuel tank and rupturing the hydraulic system. Following the adage that if you are hit by ground fire you're flying too high, 'Pop' dropped lower and his prop struck a runway. Although the blades were bent back about two feet at each tip, and with the aircraft vibrating severely, he succeeded in limping back to Manston.

On 12 May the 359th was assigned to penetration, target and withdrawal support for B-17s bombing the synthetic oil plant at Merseburg, in Germany (the group provided escort to Merseburg seven times). R/V was over Fulda, in Germany, and the bombing results were noted to be good. At 1420 hrs, before dropping escort, Red Flight of the 369th, led by Capt Ettlesen, with two P-51s from Yellow Flight as top cover, broke off and made a 600-mph dive towards an airfield at Thamsbruck. Hitting the deck three miles out, the four P-51s lined up for the attack. Lt D H Laing 'flamed' one twin-engined aircraft and Ettlesen destroyed another, which he shared with Lt Robert Thacker, and damaged a second.

During the course of the attack, Thacker actually cut across Ettlesen's line of fire and received three holes in the tail of his Mustang for his trouble! Lt Herbert C Burton hit a flagpole during the attack, wrenching the wing on his Mustang, although he returned safely to base.

On 15 May four P-51s were ordered to be kept on alert against possible German paratroop attacks on East Wretham. At about this time, VIII Fighter Command extended a pilot's tour of duty from 200 to 300 combat hours.

Col Tacon led the group to Berlin on the 19th, escorting a formation of B-17s – both take-off and landing in East Anglia were made in a ground fog, with hazy skies. Near Rathenow, 60 miles west of Berlin, the returning bombers were attacked by between 100 and 150 Bf 109s and Fw 190s. The 359th was so successful in breaking up the attack that no bombers were seen to go down due to enemy fighter attacks. The group, in turn, claimed 10.5 aerial kills and one damaged.

For the 370th, Lt Wetmore destroyed two Bf 109s, one of which was on the tail of a P-51. These victories took his overall score to 6.25, making him the group's second ace. Lt Paul H Bateman 'bagged' an 'Fw 190D', his gun camera film revealing the pilot bailing out, and Lt Charles W Hipsher damaged a Bf 109. The 370th resumed its bomber escort after the combat.

For the 369th, Lt Herbert Burton caused the collision and disintegration of two Bf 109s during a head-on attack, Lt Charles H Kruger destroyed a Bf 109 that was on the tail of a P-51, Lt Robert Thomson destroyed a Bf 109 from which the pilot bailed out and Lt Ettlesen shared in the destruction of a Bf 109 with a pilot from the 352nd FG. Ettlesen's shared victory was

'Pop' Doersch struck the runway at Reims with his propeller on 11 May 1944 and inflicted significant damage on the airscrew. Despite suffering severe vibration, the P-51B kept running, and Doersch limped back to the emergency airfield at Manston, on the Kent coast. Aside from the damage to the propeller, the Mustang had also been hit in the right wing by an explosive 20 mm shell, which had drained a nearby fuel tank and ruptured the fighter's hydraulic system

hard-earned, with the combat starting at 23,000 ft and the German having the advantage.

As they worked down to tree-top level, the only gun on Ettlesen's P-51 that was still firing ran out of ammunition, and he considered ramming the Bf 109. The pilots exchanged stares before the Mustang was caught in the Messerschmitt's prop wash, causing Ettlesen to hit a tree, damaging the fighter's wing and oil cooler. At that moment Lt Ed Zellner of the 328th FS/352nd FG finished the Bf 109 off. Ettlesen struggled back to base with only eight pounds of oil pressure.

Lt John Oliphint also participated in a drawn-out engagement with a Bf 109, repeatedly scoring hits as his target shed parts. He pulled in closer, and with the next burst the German fighter sprayed fuel and oil all over his Mustang. As Oliphint rolled past his foe, his propeller sliced off the Bf 109's left aileron. 'Ollie' then pulled up alongside the Messerschmitt, their wings overlapping. He recalls;

'The pilot was shot to pieces, dying in the cockpit, trying to stuff his scarf into a hole in the left side of his chest at the shoulder. One of my 0.50-calibre armour-piercing bullets must have hit him there. He felt my propeller hit his left wing tip and he looked at me. I sat there dumbfounded as he slowly pulled off his helmet, looked straight into my eyes and saluted me. I nodded my head at him and steered clear. This was the finest moment of my career as a fighter pilot.'

19 May 1944 was a busy day for the 359th, with its pilots claiming 10.5 kills during a huge engagement 60 miles west of Berlin. Top scorers on this day were Lt Herbert C Burton (above) of the 369th FS and Lt Ray Wetmore (right) of the 370th FS, both of whom claimed two Bf 109s apiece. Seen here being carried by his groundcrew after the mission, Wetmore's double haul made him an ace. Ex-33rd FS pilot Burton would finish his 49-mission tour (in August 1944) with 3.5 kills to his credit

The Bf 109 rolled over and the pilot dropped out. 'Ollie' followed him down and saw him hit the ground.

The 369th lost Lt D H Laing (in P-51B 42-106893) near Berlin when his engine quit and he bailed out, becoming a PoW. On a more positive note, the 368th's Lt Raymond Janney III was credited with a Bf 109 destroyed, as was Capt Charles Mosse. The latter pilot also downed two more Messerschmitts, but he was never given credit for these. His sole official victory was witnessed by his wingman, and the remaining two occurred minutes later when he exited cloud cover directly behind a pair of Bf 109s. Both German pilots bailed out after their fighters were hit.

About 50 miles north of Berlin, alone, and low on fuel, Mosse set a course for home. Minutes later a Bf 109 attacked him from below. 'His first shot exploded on the left side of my cockpit, knocking the throttle quadrant out of my hand and filling the cockpit with fire and smoke. I jettisoned the canopy, released my seat belt and gave the control stick a sharp push down.'

Mosse was left sitting in mid-air, and as he floated down in his 'chute the German buzzed him and waved. After landing safely and walking north for about ten minutes, he was taken prisoner by a German paratrooper, who escorted him to a nearby airfield where he was treated for burns around the wrists and eyes. A few days later Mosse arrived at a PoW camp, which he shared with 2000 other Allied airmen. As for the two Bf 109s he shot down, he never filed a claim. 'I was just getting the job done,' he said.

The 368th FS's Lt James B Smith was also shot down on 19 May in P-51B 42-106804. He too became a PoW.

As these early actions reveal, the 359th's P-51B/Cs, like those of other groups in VIII Fighter Command, suffered from frequent gun jams due to the canted installation of the fighter's four 0.50-cal Brownings. Field work eased the problem, but 368th FS armourer Larry Lovell exposed a major fault with the individual weapons fitted to many of his squadron's Mustangs. He stated that the machine guns manufactured by Kelsey Hayes, under contract from Browning, were of inferior quality. Indeed, even after a lot of reworking they would still jam after firing just a few rounds. The problem was so bad that crates of Kelsey Hayes replacement guns were not accepted by the 368th.

However, careful attention to the loading of ammunition by armourers paid big dividends, as was demonstrated in the group's June 1944 records which revealed that just one gun stoppage was reported among the 368th's P-51B/Cs, and 3410 rounds were expended.

Capt Charles Mosse and his Scottish wife Nina. Mosse, who was shot down by a Bf 109 over Germany on 19 May 1944 minutes after downing a trio of Messerschmitt fighters, had met Nina while visiting family friends in Scotland. He would remain a PoW until war's end

On 21 May Lt Col Swanson led the 359th on a dedicated train strafing mission (dubbed a *Chattanooga* mission after a popular song at the time) to Ratzeburg, in Germany. The results of the ensuing action are broken down by squadrons;

370th FS

At 1230 hrs, on an airfield near Schwerin, Lt Robert Callahan destroyed one Ju 88 and damaged another and Lt Warren R Newberg damaged two Ju 88s. The most successful strafer, however, was Lt Joseph E Shupe, who destroyed four Junkers bombers and damaged three more – he had already claimed two aerial victories and a strafing kill prior to this mission. During the attack, Shupe's ventral scoop struck the ground and his Mustang (P-51B 42-106921) was hit by ground fire. He gained enough altitude to bail out, and although he was listed as missing in action, it was later learned that Shupe had been killed. Other 370th claims included one twin-engined training aircraft destroyed, two locomotives destroyed and two damaged, and damage to two switch houses, one water tank, two round-houses, two railway stations and three radar installations.

369th FS

At 1235 hrs, near Klutz, Capt Richard H Broach and Lt Robert B Sander shared in the destruction of a single-engined aircraft that crashed in a field. From 1240 hrs and 1325 hrs, between Lübeck and Schwerin, Lt Eugene R Orwig Jr destroyed a twin-engined transport and damaged another parked on a grass field. It was at around this time that Lt Homer L 'Rody' Rodeheaver was killed while making a sharp turn after attacking a train near Reinfeld. His Mustang (P-51B 42-106818) went out of control and nosed in from 200 ft, exploding when it hit the ground. It is believed that

Lt Eugene R 'Rumberto' Orwig Jr and his crew chief S/Sgt Emile V Segond. Orwig's 369th FS P-51B-15 (42-106916) was named after his wife Loretta. On 21 May Orwig destroyed a twin-engined transport on the ground and damaged a second during a strafing attack on an airfield at Lubeck-Schwerin. These were the only claims he made during his 300-hour tour, which ended in July 1944. *Loretta* remained in the ETO after Orwig returned home, and the fighter was shot down by flak over St Dizier on 18 August 1944, killing its pilot, Lt Donald S Melrose

The 368th's Lt Glenn Carrol 'Batch' Bach also enjoyed his only combat successes on 21 May 1944, destroying two Fw 190s and damaging four unidentified aircraft while strafing an airfield north of Grevesmuhlen in P-51B-15 42-106867. Bach flew 102 missions totalling 303 combat hours between December 1943 and August 1944, serving initially with the 369th FS until he transferred to the 368th in January 1944. As with Capt Orwig's Mustang, Bach's P-51 was passed on to another pilot upon his departure, and it too was lost to flak, near Dreux, on 8 August. Its pilot, newly-arrived Lt John C Allen, was killed

Seen here posing with 368th FS Intelligence Officer Lt James T Burgess, Lt Arlen R 'Baldy' Baldridge was murdered after being taken prisoner on 21 May 1944

the fighter's fuselage fuel tank had not been sufficiently depleted prior to the pilot pulling hard on the controls, this surplus fuel shifting the aircraft's centre of gravity aft and rendering the P-51 tail-heavy. Other claims included 14 locomotives destroyed.

368th FS

From 1230 hrs to 1330 hrs White Flight strafed an airfield north of Grevesmuhlen, Lt Glenn C 'Batch' Bach destroying two Fw 190s and damaging four unidentified aircraft. Lt Albert G 'Aggie' Homeyer destroyed one Fw 190 and damaged a second, and Lt Robert B Hatter claimed six unidentified aircraft destroyed and three damaged for a group record. Finally, Lt Thomas S Lane destroyed two unidentified aircraft and damaged three others. Minutes later 'Aggie' Homeyer continued the destruction when he destroyed a docked seaplane at Dassow with the last of his ammunition.

Between 1245 hrs and 1315 hrs Red Flight, led by Lt Thomas McGeever, attacked an airfield near Rehna. McGeever caught a Ju 52/3m on its landing approach and sent it down in flames, and on his next pass he destroyed an unidentified aircraft on the ground. Lt Gaston M Randolph also damaged three unidentified machines at this site. Red Flight then moved on to Gadebusch and attacked railway targets. As the flight neared Wismar Lt Clyde M 'Bunky' Hudelson Jr was hit by flak (in P-51B 42-106620) and disappeared over a hill with his engine trailing smoke. 'Bunky' was listed as killed in action.

Between 1245 hrs to 1330 hrs Blue Flight, led by Lt Benjamin M Hagen III, attacked targets near Wismar. Soon after committing to his first pass, Hagen's radio failed, and he became separated from his flight. He then found an airfield being attacked by another P-51 from the 359th, and joining in the gunnery pattern, he destroyed one trainer and damaged two others. Meanwhile, the rest of Blue Flight, consisting of Lts Olin P Drake, Arlen R 'Baldy' Baldridge and John B Hunter, attacked an airfield in the Wismar-Rostock area. Drake damaged an He 111 and a Go 242, and as the trio of P-51s passed over a nearby field, the coolant system of Baldridge's Mustang (P-51B 43-6962) was hit by flak.

'Baldy' made a safe crash-landing and ran towards a forest as Drake strafed his still intact P-51. The downed pilot was quickly intercepted by a soldier on a motorcycle, and then taken by an SS *Sturmfuhrer* called Peters to the courthouse at Bad Doberan. After being brutally beaten, Lt Baldridge was shot through the heart by a police sergeant named Gosch, supposedly while 'trying to escape'. His body was taken to the cemetery morgue and Willi Selk, the cemetery caretaker, buried his remains the following morning.

35

Post-war, the area around Bad Doberan was found to have the greatest concentration of atrocity cases involving pilots ever encountered by the Theatre Graves Registration Command. By September 1948 the remains of 22 American and two British pilots had been discovered there.

Early on the morning of 22 May a German nightfighter downed an RAF Lancaster near to the 359th FG's Service Company area. Only the tail gunner, who was found still clutching his guns, survived the crash.

On the 23rd Col Tacon led the first mission as the group laid on penetration, target and withdrawal support for B-17s bombing the marshalling yards at Metz, in France. Lt Col Swanson led a second mission, dive-bombing a railway bridge at Hasselt, in Belgium. This operation marked the combat debut of the Merlin-powered P-51 as a dive-bomber. The strike force was made up of 103 Mustangs from the 359th and 361st FGs, 89 of which carried two 500-lb bombs apiece. The remaining 14 aircraft provided fighter escort. Seventy-five of the Mustangs scored hits on the bridge, completely demolishing it – for the group to achieve 84 per cent accuracy on its first dive-bombing mission revealed just how skilled the pilots of the 359th FG were.

On 24 May Maj Clifton Shaw led the group in a B-17 escort to Berlin. Shortly after taking off, the P-51B flown by Lt Charles Kruger of the 369th FS developed an engine oil leak that obscured his vision, forcing him to make an emergency landing. The impact caused the right drop tank to explode, enveloping the Mustang in flames, but Kruger escaped serious injury.

R/V was made near Neumünster, in Germany, and escort was dropped at 1110 hrs north-west of Berlin, where the 368th and 369th engaged 25 or more Bf 109s. Lt John B Hunter of the 368th and Lt Virgil E Sansing of the 369th shared the only kill. Lt Thomas McGeever of the 368th, and

This take-off crash involved the 369th FS's Lt Charles H Kruger and his brand-new P-51B-10 42-106629, christened *Nancy June 2nd*. The accident occurred on 24 May 1944 when the pilot's vision was obscured by an oil leak soon after departing East Wretham. When he set back down on the grass runway, the impact caused the right drop tank to explode. Kruger escaped the inferno, and went on to complete his tour, scoring two aerial kills

Ray Wetmore scored four aerial kills in P-51B-15 42-106894 – two Bf 109s on 19 May (to give him ace status) and two Fw 190s ten days later. His scoreboard details all his victories up to June 1944, and those crosses marked with a 'G' in the centre denote ground kills. Note that the exhaust shrouds have been removed from this aircraft. Although rear vision was not good in the P-51B, several pilots preferred the early model's higher top speed in comparison with the 'bubble-top' P-51D. The quoted top speed of the B-model was 440 mph, but test figures cranked it up to 457 mph

three flights from the 369th, then strafed targets from Stendal to south of Berlin.

On 25 May the field order for the day's mission arrived so late that the group was 30 minutes behind schedule on take-off. Col Tacon led the Mustangs aloft as they rushed to provide target and withdrawal support for B-24s raiding the marshalling yards at Mulhouse, in France.

The 359th arrived just as the bombers were leaving the target, and minutes later the engine of Capt Ettlesen's P-51C (42-103354) suffered a flak hit at 25,000 ft over nearby Saarbrücken, in Germany. Turning due south, he covered 25 miles before bailing out near Sarrebourg, in France. Ettlesen evaded capture and joined the *Maquis* (French resistance), and upon finally returning to England in August, he learned that his mother had committed suicide, believing him to be dead.

Lt Col Swanson led the 359th on the 29th as the Group provided penetration, target and withdrawal support for B-24s targeting Politz, in Germany. At 1200 hrs the 370th was cruising at 30,000 ft in its assigned escorting position, with the 368th and 369th about 15 miles behind, when about 60 German fighters attacked the lead box of bombers. Two B-24s were seen to go down as the bandits cut through the formation and continued on in a high-speed dive.

All three squadrons of the 359th chased after the fighters and engaged them over Stettin. For the 370th, Capt Raymond Lancaster destroyed one Bf 109 (its pilot was filmed hanging in his parachute) and was awarded a second as a probable, Lt Howard E Grimes 'bagged' two Fw 190s destroyed, with one of the pilots bailing out, and CO Lt Col Murphy was credited with one Focke-Wulf destroyed and one shared with Lt Doersch. The latter pilot claimed two shared Fw 190 kills (the second with Lt Robert W Siltamaki), which were enough to make him the 359th FG's third ace. Squadronmate Ray Wetmore's two Fw 190 victories boosted his tally to 8.25 kills, making him the group's leading ace – a position he would hold until war's end.

Meanwhile, the pilots of the 369th FS were also seeing action, Lt Robert Thacker chasing an Fw 190 from 23,000 ft down to the deck with an indicated airspeed of more than 600 mph. At 8000 ft he successfully began pulling out of the dive using both arms, but the Fw 190 failed to recover. The unit's leading ace, Lt Robert Booth, destroyed his eighth, and last, kill of the war when he hit a Focke-Wulf from close range. Pieces from the disintegrating fighter put five dents in his P-51 and cracked the windscreen. The Fw 190 was left in a spiralling vertical dive, trailing grey smoke.

The 369th had two pilots killed during the fight, however, Lts Lowell W 'One-Eye' Brundage (in P-51B 42-106691) and Myron C Morrill Jr (in P-51B 42-106913) last being seen chasing five Fw 190s near Malchin.

For the 368th, Lts Robert B Hatter and Benjamin M Hagen destroyed one Bf 109 each – Hagen reported that his quarry was painted black overall. With the encounter over, the 359th resumed escort until relieved by P-38s near Schleswig, in Germany.

Col Tacon led on 30 May as the group flew penetration, target and withdrawal support for B-17s pounding aircraft factories near the German town of Dessau. R/V was made over Einbeck at 1048 hrs, and 12 minutes later the 369th engaged ten Bf 109s 50 miles west of Dessau, although no claims were made on this occasion.

During the encounter Lt Booth's engine started cutting out so he lost height and headed for home. He hit a few targets along the way, damaging a Ju 88, a locomotive, an armoured car and an oil derrick. Booth then escorted a returning, crippled B-17 until it was brought down by flak at 1215 hrs near Lathen. He saw only two parachutes.

At 1115 hrs, 20 miles west of the target, enemy fighters slashed through the 'Forts', and the 368th and 370th chased after the bandits.

For the 370th, Lt Howard Grimes claimed one Bf 109 destroyed, which he shared with Lt Charles Hipsher. The latter pilot also shared in a second kill with Lt Siltamaki. The pilots bailed out of both German fighters. The 368th's Lts Robert W Hawkinson and John Hunter also shared in the destruction of a Bf 109, which broke up while trying to crash-land.

On the way home Capt Richard H Broach of the 369th strafed a barge near Tiel and left it burning. He then attacked a train, but took a 20 mm hit in an oil line. Coaxing his overheating fighter (P-51B 42-106771) in the direction of the North Sea, Broach forced landed south-west of Amsterdam. After setting his P-51 alight he hid in the backyard of a farmhouse, where he was found three hours later by the Germans and taken prisoner.

Lt Col Swanson led the first of two missions on 4 June, the group providing area support for B-17s and B-24s pounding coastal defences in the Pas de Calais. Forty-three P-51s headed off and only one returned early. No bombers were lost and no contact was made with the Luftwaffe.

At 1452 hrs a radio transmission was heard from Lt Emer Cater of the 368th, the pilot stating that he had lost oil pressure and was bailing out (of P-51B 43-6491). He parted company with his aircraft over the Straits of Dover, 20 miles south-east of Folkestone, and Lt Earl P Perkins of the 368th and Lt John S Marcinkiewicz of the 370th followed him down until he reached the water. Three Spitfires, four Thunderbolts, a Warwick and two launches were on the scene almost immediately, but all they found was an oil slick, a seat cushion and a half-inflated dinghy.

The second mission of the day was an uneventful penetration, target and withdrawal support for B-24s hitting airfields and a marshalling yard near Paris.

On 5 June the 359th was released for training and maintenance. All passes were stopped, telephones leading off the base cut off, and the civilians on East Wretham forbidden from leaving. The groundcrews began painting invasion stripes on the Mustangs.

D-DAY

On 6 June 1944 the long-awaited invasion of France began, and during the course of the day the 359th FG flew six missions. The briefing for the first operation was called at about 0200 hrs, and before boarding the trucks that would take them out to their Mustangs, the pilots gathered around Capt Wilbur C Zeigler, the Station Chaplain, for the pre-mission prayer. The rain suddenly stopped and the clouds parted, revealing a bright moon that lit up the entire base. Zeigler also noted that there was not a sound anywhere. In his monthly morale report, he called this 'one of the holiest moments of my life'. It was a sentiment not lost on those present.

The first mission on that historic day began at 0242 hrs, when Col Tacon led an area patrol of Normandy. No contact was made with the enemy.

The second mission – escorting bombers hitting targets on the French coast – got under way at 0554 hrs, under the leadership of Lt Col Murphy. Five hours later, as the 359th flew at 25,000 ft over Chateau Thierry, in France, four Fw 190s were spotted at 8000 ft. The 368th's White Flight dived towards the bandits, and quickly discovered there were about 20 enemy aircraft in the area. The German fighters escaped by diving into cloud cover.

Long before the P-51s assigned to the second mission returned home, Lt Col Tyrrell led 12 Mustangs dive-bombers against railways and roads around Le Mans. Mission number four, led by Maj Niven Cranfill, involved 15 aircraft attacking ground targets around the French town.

At 1318 hrs Maj Daniel McKee took 11 P-51s on a dive-bombing mission around Le Mans, and minor damage was inflicted on two railway bridges west of the town.

The sixth, and last, mission of D-Day was launched at 1805 hrs, led by Lt Col Swanson – all three squadrons too part. West of Le Mans, the 369th's Red Flight, consisting of Lts Herbert Burton (Red 1), Robert

Capt Wilbur C Zeigler was the Station Chaplain at East Wretham. At the beginning of the 359th's operations, the 67th Fighter Wing (FW) issued an order forbidding pre-mission prayers in the briefing room. This came about because another chaplain had tried to prepare a group of pilots to face their deaths, whereupon they refused to fly that day's mission! Col Tacon pointed out that the order read 'in the briefing room'. Henceforth all pre-mission prayers were conducted outside

This 368th FS P-51D-5 was flown by Col Tacon on D-Day. Note that its stripes were neither parallel or plumb. 44-13404 was shot down by an enemy fighter on 12 September 1944, killing pilot Lt Louis E Barnett (*Robert Hatter*)

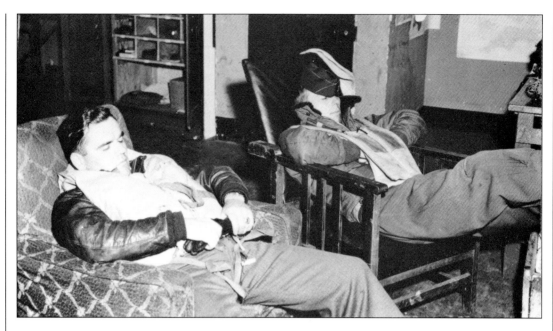

Capt Robert Laughry Pherson of the 369th FS (foreground) and Lt Robert H Addleman of the 368th FS enjoy a nap between missions on D-Day. Pherson was killed by an Fw 190 west of Paris on 12 June 1944 after chalking up 240 combat hours and two aerial kills. Addleman completed his tour in November 1944

Lt Harry 'Cuz' Cuzner Jr of the 369th FS. On D-Day 'Cuz' teamed up with squadronmates Oliphint and Pherson to wreak havoc on enemy rail targets. Note how the gunsight fitted to Cuzner's P-51C-10 (42-103793) has been covered over so as to allow this photograph to be taken. The pilot finished his 300-hour tour in September 1944

Booth and Gilbert R Ralston Jr, attacked rail targets. They shared claims of two locomotives and eight to ten oil tank wagons destroyed, and damage to a German army truck and a radio tower.

East of Le Mans Yellow Flight of the 369th, also consisting of three P-51s piloted by Lts Robert Pherson (Yellow 1), John Oliphint and Harry F 'Cuz' Cuzner Jr, attacked rail targets. At 2010 hrs the flight made several passes on ten trucks near Conlie, but the vehicles refused to burn. With the defensive ground fire becoming more intense, the pilots moved on to Biele, where between 30 and 40 ammunition wagons were spotted on a siding. Oliphint and Cuzner quickly destroyed two of them, which derailed the others and started fires, wrecking the siding and mainline tracks. Strafing the remaining wagons started a series of explosions that completely destroyed the adjacent tracks and nearby warehouses.

During one of his passes, Oliphint's Mustang was enveloped in the flames from an exploding wagon and hurled from an altitude of less than

100 ft to more than 1000 ft, where he witnessed a wheel from a wagon hurtling past his wing! On returning to base, Oliphint discovered that the paint on the underside of his P-51 had been singed, with dents in both wings and tail. A chunk of wood was also lodged next to the landing light. However, the Mustang was back flying the next day. The 359th's 'Longest Day' ended at 2315 hrs. It had been exhausting for everyone involved.

A dive-bombing and strafing assignment in the Le Mans area was the first of three missions flown on the 7th. The 370th took off at 0439 hrs and returned 15 minutes later because of bad weather. At 0638 hrs they were off again, with Lt Col Murphy leading. At 0756 hrs Lt Robert M Borg attacked a line of wagons on a railway siding outside La Flèche, in France. He placed two 500-lb bombs under the centre wagon and ten of them exploded.

Four minutes later Red, White, Blue and Yellow Flights attacked an armoured convoy north of Le Mans – five light tanks, six vehicles and two signal trucks were destroyed, with a further 30 tanks and trucks damaged. The 359th was back on the ground at East Wretham by 1000 hrs.

Nineteen minutes later the second mission (area support for B-17s and B-24s hitting targets in north-west France) was airborne. This trip was flown by the 368th and the 369th, and no bombers were lost and no contact was made with the Luftwaffe. On the way home, the 368th strafed nine locomotives, 100 wagons, a roundhouse and three trailers carrying ammunition that exploded. Lt John S Marcinkiewicz's Mustang (P-51B-10 42-106667) was damaged by debris from one of the trailers and his engine packed up. Bailing out south-east of Fecamp, he was captured.

The third and final mission flown on the 7th (an area patrol around Tours) was up at 1738 hrs. Fires were seen at Avranches, Argentan, Domfort, Flers and Falaise in the wake of B-17 and B-24 raids in these areas. Another long day ended as the last Mustang landed at 2227 hrs.

The 359th flew three missions on the 8th, the first of these being escort and area support for B-17s pounding targets around Tours. Formations came together over the town at 0759 hrs and good hits were seen on four bridges. However, the group lost two pilots – Lt Robert Sander of the 369th was killed by a German machine gunner while strafing a convoy of between 40 and 50 ammunition trucks in P-51B-15 42-106906, and Lt Benjamin Hagen III of the 368th was hit by flak while attacking a train. Hagen's Mustang (P-51B-15 42-106898) caught fire and his face and right leg were burned before he bailed out. He was captured and hospitalised, his burns blinding him for a week.

The second mission was a bombing and strafing assignment around the French town of Domfront, with all pilots returning safely. Mission three began one hour and 44 minutes later, with the pilots attacking a marshalling yard at La Flèche. When the aircraft got back to base, they had

Strictly obeying 67th FW orders, Chaplain Zeigler conducts a pre-mission prayer outside the 359th's briefing hut. Once the priest had completed his sermon, the pilots would climb aboard the trucks parked behind them and be ferried out to their fighters, in the various squadron dispersal areas

to land with the help of flares because of rain. Two pilots were missing from the 369th – Lt Oliphint (in P-51B-10 42-106679) and eight-kill ace Lt Robert Booth (in P-51B-10 43-7199), both lost to flak.

Oliphint was nearing La Flèche when his P-51 was seen to be losing coolant. He refused to turn back and pressed on to attack a train, despite the fact that his engine soon seized. His gallantry earned him a Silver Star. As his Mustang bored in, Oliphint began strafing, but his ailing fighter was quickly raked from nose to tail with 20 mm flak rounds. He recalls;

'I knew that the first shell had hit my Mustang about two feet from the front, and had blown off at least a foot of the engine cowling from what I could see. All kinds of fluids were flowing back on to the windshield. The second shell had hit a little further back, and had blown some of the instruments out of their panel, and they were scattered all over the cockpit. Shattered pieces of glass from the instruments had flown all over and stuck into every exposed area of my face and hands. A third 20 mm shell had exploded inside the cockpit, with some 14 pieces of shrapnel hitting me in the head, face, neck, shoulder, arm and legs.

'One whole panel had blown out of the canopy on the right side, and pieces shot out the other side. The canopy frame was warped and bulged tightly shut. The fourth, fifth and sixth shells exploded behind the cockpit about a foot or two apart, and I did not have time to look or think about the damage they had inflicted.'

Oliphint released his bombs point blank into the side of the locomotive, and the then lightened fighter zoomed over the train, glided silently over a German anti-aircraft gun and its wide-eyed crew, and crashed some distance further on. The impact tore off both wings, sheared off the tail and buried the engine and cockpit in mud. The next morning Oliphint was dug out by the *Maquis*, but they reported his position to the German army so that he would receive proper medical attention. However, it was the Gestapo who took him prisoner.

After being interrogated and tortured, Oliphint, with the help of a few inmates, made a daring escape, but only after killing the German doctor who had refused to treat his wounds by cutting his throat with a razor. Oliphint made his way to the nearest railway station, where he was forced to kill a German soldier before escaping again and joining the *Maquis*.

During his stay with the Resistance fighters, Oliphint gathered data for British intelligence, often by riding the roads on a bicycle and playing the part of the village idiot. During a night raid he and the *Maquis* sneaked on to an enemy airfield and tried to steal a Bf 109, but in the dark and unfamiliar layout, he succeeded only in retracting the landing gear! His frustration in failing to steal the fighter was eased when the raiders blew up nine aircraft.

One night in August Oliphint was picked up by a Lysander, which in turn almost fell victim to a German nightfighter whilst on its return flight to England. Oliphint later learned that the data he had collected was used by Gen George Patton during his famous late summer break-out from Normandy.

The rigorous pace continued, with the 359th flying four missions on 10 June. The first started at 0708 hrs, and saw fighters providing escort and area support for B-24s hitting targets around Rouen. After its job was done the group went strafing.

East Wretham's resident Westland Lysander, operated by an RAF detachment as a general communications hack. Dubbed the 'Lizzie' by the British, the rugged aircraft was used for weather reconnaissance, dropping supplies and picking up agents from behind enemy lines. A Lysander was also used to retrieve John Oliphint from occupied France in mid-August 1944 (*Palicka*)

One hour and 13 minutes after the first mission ended, 11 P-51s of the 368th, led by Lt Col Tyrrell, provided escort for four F-5 Lightnings sent on a photo-reconnaissance mission to Antwerp, in Belgium. Their target was a heavily defended marshalling yard, and after the Lightnings had made several abortive attempts to photograph the yards, 61-mission veteran Capt Wayne Bolefahr distracted the German gunners by making a daring attack on the main flak emplacements.

As the F-5s made their runs, Bolefahr's Mustang (P-51B-15 43-24786) was hit countless times, crashing through a line of trees and disintegrating as it hit the ground. Bolefahr's courage earned him a posthumous Distinguished Service Cross. On the way home, the squadron destroyed four locomotives and damaged a fifth. Many considered the Antwerp operation a suicide mission, since none of the reconnaissance aircraft previously sent to the target had returned.

The third mission of the day got under way before the aircraft on the Antwerp operation had returned. On this bombing and strafing mission to Domfront, in France, Maj Chauncey Irvine led the 369th and Lt Col Murphy led the 370th. South of St Malo, near Dinan, the force dive-bombed a railway bridge and scored several hits. At 1545 hrs White Flight of the 370th attacked a convoy of tanks near Domfront, destroying two and damaging two more. Elsewhere, claims were made for 14 trucks, two staff cars and two railway wagons, all destroyed.

The fourth and final mission saw targets near Paris bombed and strafed, Maj Niven Cranfill leading the group off from East Wretham. At 2115 hrs, between Elebuf and Louveres, the 370th destroyed four railway wagons and vast sections of track. Cranfill also attacked a heavily defended railway tunnel near Conches, the veteran pilot successfully skipping both his bombs inside.

Minutes later, the unit's Red Flight came across a Bf 109 with its wheels down. The German pilot was skilled, and he avoided being shot down by Capt Raymond Lancaster and Lt Vincent W Ambrose, who only scored a few hits between them. Lt George Doersch of the 370th then received an R/T that bandits were in the area, and he joined the fight. Latching onto a Bf 109, he fired several bursts and hit its coolant system. The pilot bailed out but his parachute failed to open.

Maj Chauncey Irvine led the 369th FS twice in 1944 – between April and late July, and then from 3 August until 17 October. He had first joined the 359th FG's 370th FS in October 1943, and remained with the unit until he transferred to Group HQ in February 1944

Meanwhile, near Evreux, Blue Flight of the 368th had just finished bombing a target when they tangled with three Bf 109s. During the fight Lt Olin P Drake (flying Col Tacon's P-51C-5 42-103329) forced two of the German fighters to crash, but the third machine latched on to his tail. A burst of 20 mm fire from the Bf 109 blew a large hole in the Mustang's left wing root, and also hit the engine. In a chivalrous gesture the German pilot flew formation with Drake until he made a safe crash landing, and then circled overhead before leaving. The American avoided capture and was hidden by the French, along with S/Sgt Melvin Curry, a B-17 ball turret gunner who had also recently bailed out. Both were liberated by US forces and returned to England in September.

The operational pace slowed on 11 June, with the 359th flying just two missions. The first was a penetration escort for B-26s headed for Paris, after which the group dive-bombed and strafed a marshalling yard south-west of Amiens. On the return flight Lt Gilbert Ralston of the 369th was hit by flak near Compiègne and wounded in the belly. Bailing out (of P-51B-5 43-6620) five miles off the French coast, he found that his dinghy was missing its inflation bottle, but his Mae West kept him afloat until he was picked up by an Air Sea Rescue Walrus 30 minutes later. Fired on by German coastal batteries, and unable to take off, the underpowered and overloaded Walrus had to taxy back across the English Channel.

The second mission of the day saw targets around Vire/St Martin, in France, singled out for bombing and strafing attacks. The 368th lost Lt William R Simmons to flak during an attack on Bretteville, his Mustang (P-51B-5 43-6775) crashing near Maltot. One of the unit's original pilots, Simmons did not survive.

On the 12th Col Tacon led target and withdrawal support for B-17s hitting airfields around Paris. The fighters remained with the bombers as far as the French coast, where the 359th turned back to strafe targets of opportunity west of Paris. White Flight of the 369th attacked two light flak positions, then came across a fight between P-51s and Fw 190s (which were evidently taking off because their landing gear was still down).

Maj Chauncey Irvine fired a burst at a Focke-Wulf that was about to attack a P-51 that was already on fire and in the process of bellying in. Two Fw 190s then jumped on Irvine's tail and began firing. Firewalling the engine in his Mustang, he headed for home, noticing that his pursuers had neglected to retract their landing gear. While exiting the area, Irvine crossed the airfield for the last time, strafing a hangar housing a Bf 109, then a light tower. The Germans abandoned the chase and Irvine carried on home.

Moments after White Flight had used up most of their ammunition strafing, they were jumped by eight Fw 190s. In the vicious mêlée that ensued, Capt Robert Pherson was killed (in P-51B-15 42-106848) and Lt Howard A Linderer shot down (in P-51B-10 42-106649) and taken prisoner.

Lt Leroy D Hess Jr evened up the score when he downed two Fw 190s, but while in pursuit of a third Focke-Wulf, which he damaged, his Mustang (P-51B-15 42-106841) was hit by flak over the Fw 190s' base. Hess bellied his fighter in and was quickly taken prisoner. Several days later Hess was interrogated by a German officer, who showed him a group photo of the 359th's pilots. The officer, who had lived in America for a number of years pre-war, boldly told his prisoner that he had been promised Cincinnati, Ohio, when the war was over!

The 369th's Lt Leroy Hess Jr fought a losing battle with a gaggle of Fw 190s in a flak-damaged P-51B west of Paris on 12 June 1944. He succeeded in downing two of his foes before force-landing his Mustang near Versailles and was captured

The weather dawned bright and clear on 15 June, and the 359th was assigned to withdrawal support for B-17s raiding the marshalling yards at Angoulême, in France. The group was back at East Wretham by 1140 hrs, and the pilots and groundcrews were able to grab a much-needed rest. At noon the four-fighter alert flight, maintained since May, was abolished.

Four days later the group mounted penetration, target and withdrawal support for B-17s striking at airfields around Bordeaux. Two fighter groups turned back early because of cloud layers extending to 29,000 ft, although the 370th and two flights from the 369th pressed on and made R/V over Cholet. The bombing was considered a great success. Lt Doersch lost the use of his flight instruments during the mission, and returned to base using his escape kit compass after an amazing 7.5-hour flight.

Lt Col Swanson led the 359th on the first of two missions on the 20th, the group escorting for B-24s sent to bomb oil facilities at Politz, in Germany. R/V was north of the German island of Heligoland at 0801 hrs and 25,000 ft. At 0920 hrs, near Putbus, the bombers were attacked by about 80 rocket-firing Me 410s. The 359th was caught cold, and four B-24s were in the waters of Griefswald Bay, and a fifth was on fire and going down, before the Mustangs could break up the attack. No parachutes were spotted. After firing their rockets, the German bomber destroyers dived for the deck. These losses could have been even worse had Lts Grant M Perrin and Herbert Burton of the 369th not foiled an attack on a lone B-24. Chasing their quarry from 15,000 ft down to the ground, both men scored hits that caused the Me 410 to belly-in, shedding its right wing.

Eight days after squadronmate Leroy Hess force-landed near Versailles, Lt Virgil Sansing bailed out within several miles of where the former's P-51 had come to rest. Like Hess, Sansing had seen his Mustang struck by flak, and when the fighter burst into flames, he had no choice but to bail out. Sansing was quickly picked up by the *Maquis*, and he rejoined the 369th in September. Remaining in the Air Force post-war, Virgil Sansing commanded an F-84 group during the Korean War and flew 350 forward air controller missions over Vietnam, before retiring from the USAF in 1973

Yet another flak victim, Lt Col Albert Tyrrell (left), first CO of the 368th FS, explains how best to evade the attentions of a German fighter to Lt Joseph P Kelsey. His impromptu tutorial must have had some effect, for Joe Kelsey (formerly with the 369th FS) completed his 85-mission tour in September 1944. The same could not be said for 'Trigger' Tyrrell, who was taken prisoner on 21 June 1944 after bailing out near Berlin – he was in the process of flying his 63rd mission at the time

The second mission of the day was a strafing assignment east of Paris, led by Lt Col Murphy. When no ground targets were found in the designated area, the group flew east to Chalons and hit a marshalling yard. The 369th suffered the only loss when Lt Virgil Sansing's Mustang (P-51B-10 42-106670) was hit by flak near Versailles. The cockpit caught fire and he bailed out at 5000 ft. Sansing was picked up by the *Maquis* and was returned to Allied hands in September.

On 21 June 368th FS CO Lt Col Tyrrell led the group to Ratzeburg. There, at 0930 hrs and 29,000 ft, they met up with their charges – a batch of B-17s, which they accompanied to Berlin on a bombing raid. Of the 41 Mustangs sortied, 16 had to abort. Bombing was visual, and smoke from the target area could be seen rising to a height of 15,000 ft. The escort finished near Wittstock, after which Lt Col Tyrrell and his wingman, Lt James J Lubien, strafed an airfield east of Plau. Tyrrell destroyed an Me 410 and an Fw 189, while Lubien damaged another aircraft, despite his visibility being impaired due to flak inflicting cracks in his windscreen.

Tyrrell, who was flying P-51D-5 44-13387, was also hit, and forced to bail out – this was the first 'bubble-

top' Mustang to be lost by the 359th FG. Albert 'Trigger' Tyrell, who had been the 368th FS's first CO, and who was flying his 63rd combat mission, spent the rest of the war as a PoW.

Following the extraordinarily high number of aborts that afflicted this mission, Col Tacon had a quiet chat with those pilots who had turned back early, and the number of subsequent aborts dropped off significantly.

The 359th FG CO led a dive-bombing mission against a railway bridge at Nanteuil, in France, on 22 June, the 370th dropping 500-lb general purpose bombs. Some 24 bombs were aimed at the bridge, and a number of these actually bounced off the target without exploding. The 370th's Lt Howard Grimes (in P-51B-15 43-24791) and Lt Harold Hollis (in P-51B-15 42-106808) were killed by flak over the target. Both men had joined the squadron upon its formation in April 1943.

The following day the destination was Nanteuil, the group accompanying B-17s attacking yet another bridge. Only 13 of the 28 'Forts' dropped their loads – and they took so long doing it that the Mustang pilots were forced to turn back because of low fuel, without being able to fulfil their mission brief of providing an escort home.

Two missions were flown on 25 June, the first seeing the 359th escorting 36 B-17s that dropped supplies and OSS personnel near Saillans, in France, as part of Operation *Zebra*. At 0920 hrs each 'Fort' released 12 containers from 3000 ft, although four parachutes failed to open. The second mission sent the 359th back to Nanteuil to provide an escort for B-24s that had been given the task of trying to destroy the stubborn bridge that the Mustang pilots could not bring down on the 22nd. However, the Liberators diverted from their course and raided airfields to the south and west of Paris instead. The bridge was left standing.

Lt Elbert W Tilton (in his flying gear) of the 370th FS poses with *Mega Ann* (type and serial unknown) and its crew – S/Sgt George Dillard is on the far left. On 24 July Tilton downed a German Fieseler Fi 156 communications aircraft, and he followed this up on 9 August with a Bf 109 destroyed. These were his sole aerial victories prior to the completion of his tour in January 1945

By the end of June, 15 P-51Ds had been delivered to East Wretham, and only 46 of the original 86 pilots that had left the US with the 359th FG remained on flying status.

Multiple missions returned on 6 July, the first seeing the group completing a run to the port city of Kiel, in Germany, looking after B-24s bombing the shipyards. It was hard to see how successful the raid had been because heavy smoke hid the target, and on the return flight, 39 miles north of Borkum Island, several fighter pilots saw nine airmen bail out of a B-24. Tacon and his section circled the area for two hours and 40 minutes, calling air-sea rescue for help. They dropped their empty fuel tanks for the crew to cling onto, but by the time an RAF Coastal Command Wellington arrived and dropped a dinghy, all nine men were dead.

The second mission was uneventful area support for B-17s and B-24s bombing *Noball* sites in the Pas de Calais and rail targets south of Paris.

The group was scheduled to fly to Munich on the 13th, providing full mission escort for B-17s. However, East Wretham was 'socked in', and the 359th only launched in time to provide withdrawal support. Shortly before R/V, Lt Thomas Lane of the 368th reported that his Merlin was losing power and turned back, with Lt John S Keesey as escort. Over the Channel, near Bradwell Bay, Lane's engine started smoking badly, and he bailed out at 800 ft. Twenty minutes later he was picked up by an air-sea rescue launch.

Meanwhile, the group made R/V, and shepherded the bombers back to England. Lts Wilson K Baker Jr, Robert Callahan and James H O'Shea of the 370th escorted two straggling B-24s from another raiding force, with wounded aboard. They 'ran interference' to draw flak, then radioed course changes to the bombers so they could avoid further punishment. O'Shea took the B-24 he was escorting to the English mainland before he headed home, while Baker and Callahan guided their crippled charge to Manston. The bomber crews later telephoned and wrote letters of appreciation to the trio, who were recommended for the Air Medal.

Maj Chauncey Irvine was in charge of the first mission on the 14th, which saw the group escorting B-17s returning home after dropping supplies and equipment to troops involved in Operation *Cadillac* in southern France. The second mission was an escort for a routine weather reconnaissance flight.

Lt James H O'Shea claimed a solitary aerial victory (an Fw 190 on 10 September 1944) during his combat tour with the 370th FS, which he completed in December 1944. He was one of three pilots from the unit recommended for an Air Medal after they escorted two damaged B-24s back to England on 13 July 1944

Operations on 21 July began with some harsh words from Col Tacon during the 0630 hrs briefing, as he took a hard line on aborts, and those who generally shirked their duty.

The 359th then divided into 'A' and 'B' groups for a double escort mission to Germany. 'A' group looked after B-24s as they hit Oberpfaffenhofen, while 'B' group journeyed to Munich with the 'heavies'. R/V for 'B' group was near St Wendel, in Germany, at 0924 hrs, and 0926 hrs for 'A' group. One bomber was seen to explode over Munich due to flak, and other crews watched in vain for parachutes to appear.

Some 75 enemy fighters attacked the bombers in the target area at 1040 hrs, and Lt Col Murphy led his section through the flak over Munich to intercept them. All but one of the Bf 109s dived for the deck, the sole remaining Messerschmitt pilot being intent on hammering down a B-24, which he duly set on fire before making his escape. Three parachutes were spotted from the doomed Liberator. Murphy followed the Bf 109 down in a high-speed dive to below 10,000 ft, where he hit it hard and the German pilot bailed out.

On the way home, Yellow Flight of the 370th strafed an airfield at 1110 hrs north of Landsberg. Flt Off Walter W Wiley destroyed one Ju 88 and damaged ten others, plus two oil storage tanks and a locomotive, Lt Robert Siltamaki destroyed one Ju 52 and three He 111s, as well as damaging two unidentified twin-engined aircraft, and Flt Off Luther C Reese claimed another Ju 88 destroyed. Reese's and Siltamaki's P-51s were both hit by 20 mm fire, the latter's fighter (P-51B-1 43-12147) being struck in the coolant system, then an oil line. Its Merlin ran for just one minute before it seized, and Siltamaki hit his head on the gunsight when he crash-landed. Stumbling into nearby woods, he was eventually taken prisoner two hours later. Reese was not so lucky, for he was killed when his Mustang (P-51B-5 43-7013) crashed near Aalen.

Walter Wiley, now the sole survivor of Yellow Flight, headed for home, picking up a B-24 with two engines out en route and helping to nurse it back to England.

During the trip out, White Flight of the 368th strafed targets near Sedan, in France, claiming two locomotives destroyed and numerous railway wagons damaged. As they passed over Lille, Lt Chester Gilmore's Mustang was hit by flak, and while crossing the English Channel its Merlin started running rough. The engine finally packed up and caught fire over Kent, whereupon Gilmore rolled the fighter onto its back and bailed out near Wingham. He sustained cuts to his head and one knee, and spent a week in hospital.

On 28 July Col Tacon led as his men flew with B-17s intending to bomb synthetic oil industry refineries at Merseburg, in Germany. At 0932 hrs, near Sangerhausen, two B-17s were seen to collide, with one exploding and the other going down in a spin. Only three parachutes were counted. At 0933 hrs the target was bombed, but clouds hid the results.

At 0940 hrs the force was south of Merseburg when someone spotted contrails at 'six o'clock high'. It was an historic occasion, with Col Tacon becoming the first Eighth Air Force pilot to see Messerschmitt's rocket-powered Me 163 Komet 'in the flesh'. Five of them were spotted, and two made a diving pass at the B-17s. Tacon led his flight in an overhead frontal attack on the bandits, placing his Mustangs between the enemy and the

Capt Robert W Hawkinson of the 368th bailed out of P-51D-5 44-13386 *Miss Janet* north-east of Rouen on 2 August 1944 after his fighter had been hit by flak. Thanks to the help of local villagers, he evaded capture and was picked up by advancing Allied troops later that month

bombers. The Germans then turned into the Mustangs, and quickly passed below them before a shot could be fired. One Komet pilot continued in his dive, while the second pulled up into the sun and ignited his rocket motor. Tacon later described one of the Me 163s. 'The aircraft is a beautiful thing in the air. It was camouflaged a rust brown, similar to some of the Fw 190s, and was highly polished. It looked as if it had been waxed.' These Me 163s were on a trial flight with JG 400.

Escort was dropped at 1030 hrs, south of Gotha, and the group proceeded to strafe around Hersfeld. The 370th lost Flt Off Wiley when his Mustang (P-51B-5 43-6961) ran out of fuel ten miles south of Rotterdam. Wiley bailed out and was taken prisoner.

On 1 August the group lent a hand to Operation *Buick*, when pilots accompanied 195 B-17s dropping supplies to the *Maquis* in southern France. As the 368th left the drop zone, Lt Elby J Beal's Mustang was hampered by a runaway prop at 11,000 ft. With the Merlin running between 3500 and 3800 rpm (red line is 3000) it started smoking heavily, and Beal landed at a P-47 base in Normandy. The following day his P-51 was fitted with a new engine and propeller governor, and Beal returned safely to East Wretham.

The following day the 359th, led by Lt Col Swanson, made rendezvous over Coburg, France, with B-17s heading for fuel dumps near Paris. The results of the bombing were good, and after seeing the 'heavies' safely out to the coast, the 359th turned back to carry out a strafing assignment around Rouen. White Flight of the 368th, led by Capt Robert W Hawkinson, followed a railway looking for a target when they spotted an army truck. As the flight attacked the vehicle, three flak positions cut loose on them and Hawkinson's Mustang (P-51D-5 44-13386) was badly hit.

He pulled up to 800 ft and bailed out north-east of Rouen. Breaking an ankle on landing, the pilot crawled into a hedgerow to hide. 'I soon came to a very large tree,' he remembers. 'I backed into the bushes alongside the tree. My cover was very sparse – in fact I was holding a branch in front of my face!' Hawkinson was amazed that he was not seen, as several German soldiers passed within four feet of him on their way to inspect his fighter.

The next morning he called out to a boy riding a horse, and using his phrase book, asked for civilian clothing and help to go into hiding. The boy, whose name was Gilbert Merriene, said he would help him and left. Later, another boy named Rene Dehayes brought clothes, and directed Hawkinson to a nearby wooded area, where he hid. During the night both boys returned with their uncle, a Monsieur Merriene, who was mayor of Vieux Manoir. They carried Hawkinson to the farm of another family member, where he was fed and bedded down in a barn.

Next morning he was covered with hay in the back of a horse-drawn cart driven by the mayor, and after clearing a German checkpoint, was taken to the farm of Madam Alexandrine Herbert, near Cauricourt. Hawkinson was put in a hayloft, where he remained until mid-August, when retreating German troops began filtering through the area. Fearing he might be discovered, Alexandrine moved him into her house. In late August the spearhead of a Polish armoured division arrived, and they suggested that Hawkinson remain hidden until the main body of the division caught up. A couple of days later he was picked up by a Canadian Army medical unit.

The German targets of Peenemünde and Anklam were the destinations for 4 August, as Lt Col Swanson led his men as they escorted raiding B-17s. The bombers were picked up over Kiel Bay at 1346 hrs. Large clouds of smoke were seen rising from the targets, and the flak was light. The 359th parted company with the B-17s at 1540 hrs near Eckernforde.

Five minutes later, Capt Raymond Lancaster of the 370th radioed that his Mustang (P-51D-5 44-13939) was losing oil pressure and he was heading for Sweden. Lts Richard O Rabb (in P-51B-1 43-12463) and Wilson Baker (in P-51B-5 43-6461) looked after him as far as the Swedish border, and then turned for home. At 1600 hrs they were attacked by a Bf 110, and Baker shot it down, but both pilots were now too low on fuel to return to England so they too headed for Sweden. Lancaster's P-51 was destroyed in a crash-landing after his engine quit, but Rabb and Baker landed with only 15 gallons of fuel

On 4 August 1944 Raymond B Lancaster (bottom), Wilson K Baker and Richard O Rabb (below) of the 370th FS were interned in Sweden after they were forced to land in the neutral country due to a shortage of fuel. Lancaster, a Texan, is seen posing with his first Mustang, P-51B-15 42-106805 *GALVESTON GAL*. He was flying brand-new P-51D-5 44-13939 when he came down in Sweden. Col Tacon was reportedly livid when he was told that three perfectly good aircraft, and their pilots, were gone

Capt Lester George Taylor of the 370th FS was one of eight West Point graduates to see action with the 359th FG in the ETO. Serving with the unit from April 1943 through to September 1944, he was the only 'West Pointer' to complete a full operational tour. Three were killed in action, three were captured and one died in a flying accident. Taylor scored his only kill on 5 August 1944, when he shot down an Fw 190 over Tarmstedt

left in each fighter. Col Tacon was livid when informed of the loss of three pilots and their perfectly good aircraft. Lancaster, Baker and Rabb were returned to the US a few weeks later.

The following day Maj Edwin F 'Swami' Pezda led the the 359th as it escorted B-24s sent to bomb an airfield at Halberstadt, in Germany. At 1210 hrs Red Flight of the 369th took on up to eight markingless Bf 109s between Bremen and Hamburg. Lt Frank W Holliday damaged one fighter and Lt Harold R Burt scored hits on another machine, which went into a vertical dive. He followed it down, registering 630 mph prior to pulling out at 500 ft. The Bf 109 failed to recover, hit the ground and exploded in flames.

At 1220 hrs Red Flight spotted about 20 fighters several miles away at 'nine o'clock' to the bombers and attacked. Capt Lester Taylor scored good hits behind the cockpit of an Fw 190 that went into an uncontrolled dive, its pilot probably dead. Meanwhile, White Flight made a diving attack on two Bf 109s, Maj Pezda chasing a diving Bf 109 and nailing it. As he pulled up and over the fighter, Pezda could see the pilot kicking the rudder pedals before bailing out. Lt Edwin L Sjoblad also bagged a Bf 109 and its pilot bailed out too.

Munich was the group's destination on 9 August, as Lt Col Murphy's men looked after a formation of B-17s. Following their meeting at 1006 hrs at Haguenau, in France, the weather got progressively worse as the aircraft made their way across Germany – many of the 'Forts' opted for bombing targets of opportunity instead. At 1100 hrs, near Gunzburg, just east of Ulm, the 368th tackled 30 enemy fighters that appeared head-on out of the sun. Lt John Keesey nailed an Fw 190 and the pilot jettisoned his canopy before disappearing into the clouds. Keesey was later awarded a probable. Flt Off Emory C Cook could only damage a Bf 109 despite firing off 1070 rounds of armour-piercing incendiary.

At 1115 hrs, in the same area, the 370th took on 20 Bf 109s. Lts Robert M York (who had to secure the manual high blower switch in the on position with his necktie), John W Wilson and Frank O Lux each destroyed a Bf 109 apiece, and Lt Col Murphy got an Fw 190. The latter kill gave the 370th FS CO ace status, boosting his tally to 5.75 victories. It was also a good day for future ace Lt Cyril W Jones Jr, who destroyed a Bf 109 and damaged another on his very first mission with the 370th FS.

The following day the group performed a dive-bombing mission against railway targets from Bar-le-Duc to Strasbourg, in France. The 368th attacked the marshalling yard at Bishwiller, scoring 25 hits on buildings and tracks. The squadron lost Lt Lester W Hovden in return, when he made a quick 45-degree turn to line up on his target and overstressed his Mustang's bomb-laden airframe. Both wings (of P-51B-10 42-106702) folded up and ripped off, and Hovden was killed.

The 369th's Lt Paul E McCluskey was also lost when he was shot down by ground fire (in P-51C-5 42-103743) as his unit strafed targets near Winden, in Germany. The 370th, meanwhile, attacked railway targets at Luneville, in France, and Lahr and Offenburg, in Germany. Total claims for the day included 16 locomotives, three railway carriages, one highway bridge, a switch tower and two warehouses all destroyed.

On the 13th the group flew two dive-bombing missions and an escort. It was an auspicious day for the 359th, as all three missions were completed without losses or aborts.

The 67th FW's Commanding General, Brig Gen Edward W Anderson, chose East Wretham as the fighter base to be inspected by two Soviet officers (on 9 August 1944) that were touring Army Air Force facilities in East Anglia. Seen in this official photograph taken to mark the occasion are (from left to right) unidentified, Lt Col William H Swanson (deputy Group Commander), Maj Gen Ivan Skliarov (Soviet Air Forces), Brig Gen Anderson, Maj T T Samarin (Soviet Army), unidentified and Lt Col Grady L Smith. It is ironic that seven months later the 369th would be locked in deadly combat with Soviet Yak and Lavochkin fighters near Berlin

In this still, taken from the gun camera film shot by the 369th FS's Lt Crenshaw on 10 August 1944, a locomotive's boiler ruptures after being holed by a fusillade of 0.50-cal rounds. Crenshaw's destructive habits also saw him 'make ace', with seven aerial and three ground strafing kills

On 16 August 1944 the 370th FS made history by claiming the first two Me 163s destroyed in aerial combat – a third Komet would fall before the guns of Ray Wetmore, also of the 370th, on 15 March 1945. Only five Me 163s were officially downed by P-51 pilots in the ETO, and for three of these to be claimed by the same squadron was a remarkable achievement. The first Komet destroyed was credited to Lt Col John Murphy, who was CO of the 370th from 16 March 1943 through to 1 September 1944. Murphy completed his tour with 6.25 aerial kills to his credit. Upon returning to East Wretham, his gun camera footage was quickly sent to Wing HQ for viewing by the world's press. *Stars & Stripes* also featured a series of articles about this historic combat

Minutes after Lt Col Murphy downed his Komet, his wingman, Lt Cyril Jones Jr downed a second Me 163. Jones' combat career was short but glorious, and in just 16 missions he destroyed six German fighters in the air and five aircraft on the ground. He also destroyed one locomotive and shared in the destruction of 12 more. Those who knew him said they could tell he wouldn't last long – he threw himself into battle with a total disregard for his chances of survival. Jones was killed on 12 September 1944 when his fighter was hit by flak whilst strafing an airfield south of Meindingen. He had 'made ace' just 24 hours earlier

On 16 August Lt Col Murphy was in charge of covering B-17s sent to bomb oil facilities at Bohlen, as well as an airfield at Delitzsch and aircraft factories at Halle and Schkeuditz. At 1000 hrs, near Einbeck, White Flight of the 369th was flying at 28,000 ft heading for R/V at Erfurt when three Bf 109s made a diving head-on pass at them. Maj Niven Cranfill scored hits on one, followed it down and saw it hit the ground and explode.

At 1020 hrs, just before R/V was made, Blue Flight of the 370th took on four Bf 109s. Lt Lux fired a long burst into one of them, which shed parts and began loosing coolant. He also followed the damaged fighter down, and watched as it performed 'a series of aerial cartwheels that eventually threw the pilot clean out for the cockpit'.

As the 'Forts' were being escorted south-east of Leipzig, and away from the target area, at 1045 hrs Lt Col Murphy noticed a contrail climbing rapidly towards the rear of a straggling B-17 named *The Outhouse Mouse*. It was an Me 163, and the Mustang ace overtook the rocket fighter just after it had passed the B-17. He scored several hits on the Messerschmitt before turning away in order to avoid overshooting his prey. Lt Cyril Jones Jr, who was flying as Murphy's wingman, in turn caught the Me 163 in a half-roll and fired a burst into the cockpit to secure the kill.

Meanwhile, Murphy had intercepted a second Komet, and following a long burst, an explosion blew off the top of the rocket fighter's fuselage

from the cockpit aft. Murphy's victory preceded Jones', and he became the first Allied fighter pilot to shoot down an Me 163 by just a matter of minutes. Following the stricken Komet down, Murphy spotted a second Me 163 but decided to head for England since he was alone and low on fuel. At the same time Lt Jimmy C Shoffit broke into an Me 163 that was attacking a B-17, and during a brief engagement landed hits all over its right wing. The Me 163 escaped by making a power-on dive.

Two missions were flown on the 17th, with the 359th split into 'A' and 'B' groups to carry out dive-bombing and strafing assignments in France. 'A' group hit railway targets from north-east of Rouen to Amiens.

During this mission, Lt Will D Burgsteiner of the 368th hit a tree while strafing a train and sheared six feet off the right wing of his Mustang. Blue Flight, which he was leading, escorted him home, and he made a perfect landing. Mission claims included three locomotives destroyed and 13 damaged.

Whilst the 370th was strafing trains, the 368th FS bombed an airfield at Grandvillers – the Mustangs of 'B' group had been given the area from south-east of Rouen to Beaumont. Around this time Lts Shoffit and Theophalus A Williams from the 370th were jumped by four Fw 190s near Nogent while attacking some trucks. Shoffit got in a quick shot at one of the bandits and managed to shake off a Fw 190 on his tail, despite his bombs not releasing. Williams, however, was killed when his P-51B-15 (42-106878, formerly Lt Col Murphy's mount) crashed near Rouen.

Maj Niven Cranfill led on 18 August when the group provided penetration, target and withdrawal support for B-17s heading for an airfield at St Dizier, in France. Fifty Mustangs took off and there were no aborts. The bomber formations were noted to be excellent, as were the bombing results, with ammunition and fuel dumps exploding. No B-17s were lost and no contact was made with the enemy. After the 'Forts' cleared the target area the 369th strafed the same airfield, and Lt Rene L

Almost unnoticed, Lt Jimmy C Shoffit of the 370th damaged a third Komet on 16 August. Shoffit completed his tour (in April 1945) without scoring a confirmed kill

The 368th's Lt Will Burgsteiner somehow flew this Mustang (P-51D-10 44-14062) back from Amiens, in France, after a tree sheared off six feet of its right wing. The fact that he made a gear-down landing is even more astounding. The Mustang was duly rebuilt, only to be lost following an engine fire over the Channel on 20 November 1944. Pilot Lt Merle Barth bailed out but was never found (*Page*)

Burtner destroyed three Bf 109s and one Ju 88, and damaged a Ju 52. Lt Crenshaw destroyed a second Ju 88 and a Ju 52, and damaged another Junkers bomber, while Maj Edwin Pezda damaged two more Ju 88s. Lt Donald S Melrose (in P-51B-15 42-106916) was hit by flak on his second pass over St Dizier and was duly listed as missing in action – he had been killed when his aircraft crashed near to the airfield.

Rene Burtner's fighter (P-51B-1 43-12186) was also hit by flak on the pilot's second pass. Having just strafed a water tower and a factory, he had attempted to rejoin his flight when his coolant system was hit. Going down fighting, Burtner strafed four or five gun emplacements before his P-51's engine began smoking and vibrating, and 20 miles south of St Dizier he bailed out. As he recalls;

'It was only seconds from the time I pulled the ripcord until I hit the ground. As I stood up I heard guns firing behind me. I thought, "Oh shit!", and turned around raising my arms. My aeroplane was burning fiercely in the field only a short distance away and the ammo was going off! I was in a field with a road to my left and some woods to my right. I gathered my 'chute and ran into the woods. After entering the woods I came upon a small clearing and met a man and a young boy with bicycles. They were very excited and kept saying "Boche" and pointing in a direction away to my left.

Lt Rene L Burtner of the 369th FS fell victim to flak while strafing the airfield at St Dizier on 18 August 1944. Bailing out 20 miles south of the base, he was hidden by French villagers until the area was liberated by Patton's 3rd Army just over a week later

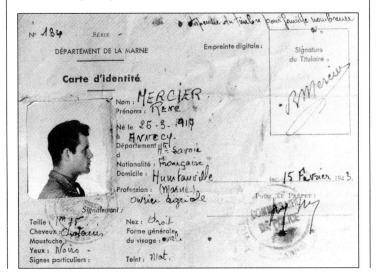

This photo shows Lt Rene L Burtner's bogus identity card, which the Resistance made for him in the name of Rene Mercier. Burtner remained with the 359th FG until September 1945, by which time he had been credited with three ground kills (*Burtner*)

Lt Lawrence A Zizka of the 370th FS scored the only aerial kill credited to the entire VIII Fighter Command on 27 August 1944. He had claimed 1.5 victories by the time he was killed in a landing accident on 1 February 1945, his Mustang (P-51K-1 44-11355) being caught in high winds on its approach to East Wretham. The aircraft crashed and exploded in woods behind the Squadron Operations Building. Zizka had been returning from a 90-minute test flight

The 370th also suffered the 359's only loss on 27 August – Lt Paul E Sundheim. He was flying at an altitude of 200 ft, looking for ground targets, when he was shot down by flak over the Netherlands. A recent arrival in the ETO, Sundheim saw out the rest of the war as a PoW

'I had completed two years of French in high school, but I could not understand what they were saying, although I knew what they meant. They gave me a bicycle and pointed me down a path that led me to a narrow dirt road. I pedalled like crazy. After probably less than a mile the road ended at a farmhouse. A man rushed up to me and took the bike and herded me into a barn. He shifted some hay around and made an area for me to hide. He left. A short time later I heard the Germans arrive, followed by loud talking. They came into the barn to search, but didn't find me.'

The French hid Burtner for more than a week before the lead elements of Gen Patton's 3rd Army arrived and Burtner joined them for two days. On the second day a convoy was sent to the rear, and Burtner was assigned as a machine-gunner on top of an escorting tank. After spending a night in Troyes, and hitching a ride to Orleans, where B-24s were flying in shipments of flour from England, Burtner managed to get on a return flight.

Escort for three RAF Warwicks searching for a downed bomber crew was the first mission flown by the 359th FG on 27 August. Visibility was poor and the flight uneventful. Maj Pezda led the second mission of the day, which saw the group accompanying B-17s sent to bomb Berlin. Heavy cloud over northern Germany saw the bombers recalled before rendezvous was made, however, and of the 371 'Forts' despatched, only 144 managed to bomb targets of opportunity.

The 359th, meanwhile, pressed on to the Münster-Osnabrück area to strafe, and the group claimed 16 locomotives destroyed and 11 damaged, plus 83 various types of railway wagons damaged. Lt Lawrence A Zizka of the 370th scored the only aerial victory by any Eighth Air Force fighter group that day when he bagged an unidentified twin-engined aircraft near Münster. The 370th also suffered the group's only loss when Lt Paul E Sundheim (in P-51B-10 42-106580) became separated from Green Flight near Münster and was later shot down by ground fire over the Netherlands. He ended up in *Stalag Luft 1*.

Lt Col Swanson led a strafing mission on the 28th that took in targets between Bar-le-Duc, in France, and Saarbrücken, in Germany. Fifty Mustangs departed East Wretham and only two aborted. One of the latter was Lt John W McAllister of the 370th, who made a dead-stick landing at Bentwaters, in Suffolk, after his engine seized. Total claims for the group included 45 locomotives destroyed and 257 railway wagons damaged. The 368th's Lt Oscar R Faldmark destroyed the only aircraft when he shot up a Ju 88 near Saarbrücken, and the 369th suffered the day's only loss when Lt Ferris C Suttle (in P-51B-15 43-24756) disappeared near Luneville, in France, and was later listed as killed in action.

The German city of Ludwigshafen was the target on 1 September, and the B-17 escort was led by Lt Col Murphy. The 359th put up 52 Mustangs (most of them D-models), and experienced only one abort. Two of the three bomber boxes aborted in response to a recall due to ten-tenths cloud cover. The third box pressed on, however, while the 359th looked in vain for them. The group was then recalled, and on the return flight the Mustang (P-51C-1 42-103318) flown by Lt Edward G Kaloski of the 368th suffered a runaway propeller followed by a loss of oil pressure. Kaloski crossed out over the French coast near Cayeux at 9000 ft, and his wingman, Lt Ray A Boyd, lost sight of the doomed fighter as Kaloski bailed out over the English Channel.

The following day Capt Benjamin H King led a six-man flight from the 368th to look for their missing squadronmate, and although visibility was reduced due to rain, Kaloski's dinghy was found and a fix made on its position. It was later learned that he had broken his leg while bailing out, paddled his dinghy five miles back to the French coast and laid on the beach for three days before being found by a fishermen. Hospitalised, Kaloski was transferred back to the US when deemed fit enough to travel.

On the 8th Mustangs of the 352nd and 359th FGs were scheduled to provide escort and top cover for the Thunderbolts of the 56th and 353rd FGs as they hammered transport targets in western Germany. Maj Pezda led the group, and of the 51 P-51s that left East Wretham, only one returned early. Some way into the mission, the 56th and 353rd radioed that they had run into a storm and could not make the R/V. At 1500 hrs the 359th began hunting targets, and two flights from the 368th strafed an airfield near Kronberg, in Germany, destroying three Ju 52s. Other claims included 33 locomotives and innumerable carriages destroyed. More than 20 trucks, one motorcycle and two half-tracks were also destroyed.

The group was tasked with looking after B-24s sent to bomb Stuttgart on 10 September, and R/V was made at 1120 hrs, just after the bombers had hit their targets. Twenty minutes later, north-west of Stuttgart, Lt Kenneth L Hobson of the 369th was diving through a light overcast at 5000 ft in search of reported bandits when he spotted two fighters. Despite being unable to jettison his drop tanks, Hobson bounced them as they broke in opposite directions.

As he was scoring hits on his first target, the second fighter crossed in front of his P-51, so Hobson broke after the latter machine and again scored hits as the pilot made evasive moves, following the terrain. While attempting to shake off the Mustang, the pilot clipped a tree with his right wing and crashed. Intent on his pursuit, Hobson realised he was being fired on by the remaining fighter. He broke, and then found he was under head-on attack, the bandit pulling up and over him. When Hobson next spotted his opponent, he was 45 degrees to the P-51's stern. He continued a hard evasive turn for two or three minutes until the bandit disappeared.

The 359th also did some strafing on the 10th, claiming three locomotives, one truck and a car destroyed. The only loss occurred when the 370th's Yellow Flight tried to beat up an airfield near Würzburg. Intense flak drove them off, but not before Lt Benjamin J Vos Jr's Mustang (P-51D-10 44-14240) was hit, crashing and burning on the airfield. Initially listed as missing in action, Vos's death was later confirmed.

This mission was significant because of the nationality of the fighters that Hobson had tangled with. His report stated that the aircraft were painted black overall, and looked similar to a P-40 fitted with B-25 twin rudders. Finally, their markings were white crosses on a red background. Clearly they were Swiss, specifically Fabrique Federale C-3603 types.

The Swiss claimed that several Mustangs had jumped them, and there had been no losses. While technically neutral, some Swiss were sympathetic to Germany, and the fact that this incident took place more than 70 miles inside German territory leads one to speculate on the intentions of the errant Swiss pilots. It should not be forgotten that treatment of American airmen interned by the Swiss improved when it became evident that Germany had lost the war!

THE 'GREATEST DAY'

The mission of 11 September 1944 is officially referred to by the 359th FG as its 'Greatest Day'. For its outstanding performance engaging superior numbers of enemy fighters while protecting the bomber formations, the group was awarded a Distinguished Unit Citation.

Capt William C Forehand led the group as it provided penetration, target and withdrawal support for B-17s raiding the German synthetic oil plants at Merseburg. The day began well, as 49 P-51s took off and only one aborted. As the 359th approached Giessen, 50+ Bf 109s were spotted flying a formation identical to that used by Eighth Air Force fighters – a tactic used with the intention of getting closer to the bombers before being discovered. The 368th broke into them before the Bf 109s could attack the 'Forts', and the Germans dived for the deck. Lt Robert E Benefiel damaged two Bf 109s while separated from his (Yellow) flight, leaving him low on fuel and forcing him to head for home. Lts Clarence M Lambright and Jack O Flack shared in destroying a Bf 109, and noticed that the other German pilots were reluctant to engage.

Down on the deck, Lambright destroyed one locomotive and shared in the destruction of two more with Flack. The latter also destroyed an oil tank wagon, before the pair headed back to England. Lt Wilbur H Lewis of Yellow Flight scored hits on a Bf 109, and he followed it in a dive that

Capt Clarence M Lambright of the 368th FS and his crew chief S/Sgt Fred W Gall pose beside Lambright's P-51D-10 44-14131. The pilot's sole victory during his tour was a Bf 109 kill he shared with Lt Jack Flack on 11 September 1944. On 18 December 1944, squadronmate Lt Paul Olson destroyed five Fw 190s with this Mustang before being shot down by flak

partially opened the P-51B's canopy, blew out the rear Plexiglas panels and broke the airspeed indicator. Busy pulling out of the dive, Lewis lost sight of his prey and was only awarded a probable. He then rejoined his flight and returned home.

At 1130 hrs, near Weimer, the 368th's Lt Arvy F Kysely destroyed a locomotive. He recalls;

'I turned in the cockpit to reorient myself for another attack on the train and immediately saw an Fw 190 fighter in front of me. I started to drop my flaps to slow down and get behind him for a quick kill, but because of my excessive speed from attacking the train, I flew up alongside and passed the Fw 190. I was so close I could see the German pilot staring at me with a puzzled look on his face like "where the hell did you come from"? Realising my predicament, I pulled up the flaps, pushed the throttle full forward and started a steep climbing turn. When I looked back at him I could see his 20 mm cannons blinking at me. They looked like 5-in artillery pieces. I had the speed and rate of climb on him so he couldn't get his nose up high enough to hit me.

'We went into a steep climbing circle for what seemed like an hour. I have no idea how long it was, probably a couple of minutes. As we went around, I knew I had to do something drastic or I would run out of gas soon, being at full throttle and rpm. Things got desperate and I kept trying to get more turn out of my aeroplane. Indeed, I tightened the turn so much that my aeroplane flipped over on its back in a snap roll. I could see the Fw 190 coming into my view through the outer ring of my gunsight as it flew through the opposite side of our turning circle. My immediate reaction was to pull the trigger. As my guns fired I could see flashes of my armour-piercing incendiary hits starting from his engine and moving aft along the fuselage to his tail. When I last saw the Fw 190, it was smoking and slowly descending.'

Alone and low on fuel, Kysely headed towards Paris, and on the way out he destroyed two German locomotives. He landed in a farmer's field near the French town of Epernay and returned home the following day.

More action took place near Mulhausen at 1140 hrs, when Red Flight of the 370th took on 30 Bf 109s and Fw 190s, effectively breaking their formation and preventing an attack on the bombers. Flt Off James O'Shea 'bagged' an Fw 190 (he reported seeing the pilot bail out) and damaged another. Lt John W Wilson also got a fighter, hitting a Bf 109 around the cockpit area and probably killing the pilot. O'Shea and Wilson then became separated, Wilson returning to base and O'Shea (in P-51D-5 44-13529) being shot down and killed by German fighters near Mulhausen.

At the same time Yellow Flight of the 369th tangled with German fighters north of Erfurt, Lt Frank Holliday downing a Bf 109 when its belly tank exploded and engulfed the Messerschmitt in flames. Like O'Shea, Holliday (in P-51D-10 44-14307) then fell victim to another Bf 109 when he was shot down and killed near Meiches. Yellow Flight member Lt John E Keur also destroyed a Bf 109, filming the pilot in his parachute. He then joined P-51s from the 357th FG and returned to England.

Five minutes after this initial clash, the remaining 369th FS pilots spotted 100+ enemy fighters five miles north of a cluster of bombers. Ignoring the daunting odds, the Mustang pilots immediately went after the German machines. Amongst the first pilots into the ranks of the enemy was Lt Grant M Perrin, who quickly destroyed two Fw 190s and scored hits on the cockpit of an Bf 109 for a probable. Lt Gilbert Ralston 'bagged' both an Fw 190 and a Bf 109, with the Focke-Wulf pilot being seen to bail out. The 369th lost Lt James F Hutton (in P-51D-10 44-14108) and Flg Off Charles R Bruening (in P-51D-10 44-14399) during the course of the engagement, both men being killed in action.

Lt Grant Michael Perrin of the 369th FS scored two kills on 11 September, and finished his 270-hour tour in January 1945 with 2.5 aerial victories and one probable

At the height of the battle, Lts James W Parsons and Joseph W 'shoot everything that moves' Mejaski became separated from Red Flight of the 369th, and while searching for their squadronmates they found a small grass airfield south of Merseburg with about 50 aircraft parked on it. The pair made five passes at the numerous Junkers bombers gathered at the site, Mejaski claiming two Ju 88s destroyed and five damaged, and Parsons one Ju 88 and one Ju 188 destroyed, as well as two Ju 88s and three Ju 188s damaged.

Thousands of feet above them, the 369th's Yellow Flight was engaging the enemy, with future seven-kill ace Lt Crenshaw downing two Bf 109s

11 September 1944 is remembered as the 359th's 'Greatest Day', for its pilots claimed 26 aircraft destroyed in the air and nine on the ground. The group paid a high price for this success, however, as four pilots were listed as missing in action and a fifth that bailed out over enemy territory evaded capture and eventually returned home. Two of those killed were Flt Off Charles R Bruening (above) and Lt James Franklin 'Hut Sut II' Hutton (left), both from the 369th FS

to open his account. One rolled over and exploded as it hit the ground, while the other crashed after the pilot bailed out. Crenshaw then destroyed a single-engined aircraft on the same field that Parsons and Mejaski had just hit. Lt Robert S Gaines Jr claimed a Bf 109 as a probable and a second damaged during a brief dogfight, while Lt Thomas J Klem damaged a Bf 109 by scoring hits on its left wing.

Blue Flight of the 370th had also seen some action when, at 1145 hrs, south of Gotha, its pilots spotted Bf 109s taking off from an airfield. Four German fighters were destroyed in the air by Lt Cyril Jones Jr, making him an ace. Lt William E Buchannon claimed a fifth Bf 109 kill. The flight then strafed the field, where Jones destroyed a Ju 88 and an He 177, and damaged two Ju 88s and two 'Me 210s'. Lt Wallace C Murray was also credited with two Ju 88s destroyed on the ground.

As this was going on, the 368th's Blue Flight encountered bandits near Halberstadt just before the bombers dropped their loads on Merseburg. Lt George F Baker 'bagged' two Fw 190s before heading home, low on fuel.

Lt Ivan B Hollomon, who was leading the 369th's Red Flight, experienced a loss of power at high altitude during the major engagement near Kölleda, forcing him to 'drop to the deck' in search of targets as he headed out. Hollomon destroyed a locomotive and damaged another, along with three wagons, near Kassel. However, he passed near an airfield and ground fire struck an oil line in his Mustang (P-51D-5 44-13689), causing the Merlin to seize near Utrecht, in the Netherlands, where he bailed out safely, evaded capture and later returned to England.

At 1202 hrs, near Eisleben, Capt Benjamin King, who was leading the 368th's Red Flight, spotted 50 fighters preparing to attack a group of B-17s from the rear. Copying the German tactics, King bounced the fighters from behind and quickly downed a Bf 109 and two Fw 190s. Two

369th FS pilot Lt Joseph W 'shoot everything that moves' Mejaski finished his 75-mission, 300-hour, tour in February 1945 with two ground kills, as well as having shared in the destruction of nine locomotives

Lt George F Baker Jr of the 368th FS and his P-51B-15 *Little Liquidator* (42-106809). Baker came tantalisingly close to 'making ace', destroying 4.5 enemy aircraft in the air, damaging another and being awarded 0.5 of a strafing kill! He completed his tour

of the German pilots were seen bailing out of their stricken fighters.

This trio of kills gave King ace status, for he had previously downed three Japanese Zero fighters whilst flying P-38s with the 339th FS/347th FG in the Pacific in 1943.

The combat took Red Flight from 27,000 ft down to the deck, where King then chased a third Fw 190, only to discover he was out of ammunition. King handed the fighter over to Lt Chester Gilmore, who made the kill.

Once all the pilots had been debriefed back at East Wretham, the 359th was credited with 26 aircraft destroyed, four probables and five damaged in the air, plus nine destroyed and 13 damaged on the ground. These victories had cost the 359th five pilots and six P-51s, however.

One 368th FS pilot who did become an ace was Capt Benjamin King, who downed a Bf 109 and two Fw 190s on 11 September 1944. The following day he 'bagged' another Bf 109, despite having two of his four guns jam. All his fighters were named after his mother, Matilda. A seasoned combat veteran, King had flown P-38s and P-39s in the Pacific in 1943 while assigned to the 339th FS/347th FG, destroying three Zeros before returning home for a rest. Aside from completing a second tour in the ETO, King also saw post-war combat in Korea and Vietnam. He retired as a brigadier general in 1971

Future ace Lt David B Archibald aborted over the Frisian Islands on 12 September 1944 and made it back to base, only to have his engine die just seconds from landing. Note the propeller stuck in the fuselage after being torn off during a cartwheel

The following day, the group was assigned escort duty for B-17s bombing oil installations at Brux, in Germany. Maj Chauncey Irvine led them off but aborted early, being replaced by Lt Jack D Stevens of the 369th. Lt David B Archibald turned back over the Frisian Islands with a rough engine (in P-51D-5 44-13545) and crashed at East Wretham when the Merlin quit just as he attempted to land. Hitting the ground hard, the fighter's right main landing gear strut snapped, causing the P-51 to cartwheel. This in turn tore off the propeller, which ended up stuck in the fuselage forward of the tail empennage. The engine was subsequently examined, and all 24 spark plugs were found to be fouled.

Back over Germany, the group pressed on to the R/V, north of Hamburg. At 1130 hrs, north-west of Berlin, Red Flights of the 368th and 369th tangled with some 50 enemy fighters making a diving attack on the B-17s. For the 368th, Capt Benjamin King claimed a Bf 109 destroyed at such close range that its coolant covered his windscreen. As the fight progressed, two of his four machine guns jammed – he was flying his assigned P-51C-10 42-103898, not the six-gun P-51D-10 44-14329 that

he had claimed three kills with 24 hours earlier. King eventually joined up with another Mustang from his flight and returned to base.

During the same engagement the 368th's Lt Merle B Barth nailed a Bf 109, forcing its pilot to take to his parachute. Lt Leonard D Carter damaged an Fw 190, then latched on to another Focke-Wulf and continued firing until it crashed. Lt Robert B Hatter damaged a Bf 109, then scored numerous hits on an Fw 190 before pulling alongside it and noticing that the pilot was slumped over the controls. The fighter crashed shortly afterwards. Hatter then caught a second Fw 190 with a solid burst, sending both it and its pilot crashing to the ground. These two kills took Bob Hatter's tally of aerial victories to three, which he added to six strafing victories scored in May. He would claim no further successes prior to ending his tour the following month.

368th pilot Lt Elby J Beal fired 480 rounds and scored only a few hits on a Bf 109 in the same engagement that Hatter achieved his double, yet the German pilot bailed out. Squadronmate Lt James H Haas of the 368th claimed his sole kill (an Fw 190) in this action, but as he pulled out of his diving attack over Pritzwalk, a wing snapped off his Mustang (P-51D-10 44-14081) and crushed his canopy. Haas bailed out through the broken Plexiglas and was duly taken prisoner.

The 368th also lost Lt Louis E Barnett (in P-51D-5 44-13404) during the course of the swirling dogfight over Wittenberge, the pilot initially being listed as missing in action. However, it was later learned that he had bailed out and that his parachute had failed to open fully. German civilians buried Barnett in a cemetery at Wutike.

The 369th also scored during this fight, with Lt Grover C Deen leading Red Flight, and he and his wingman, Lt Kenneth Hobson, engaging several Fw 190s. Deen destroyed one of the Focke-Wulfs, and then scored hits on an Me 410, before being driven off by flak. Heading back to England, he had to stop at Ghent, in Belgium, for fuel. Hobson, meanwhile, had suffered a structural failure in his Mustang (P-51D-10 44-14216) during a high-speed dive and been forced to bail out near Berlin. He was quickly captured by local authorities and was sent to *Stalag Luft 1* at Barth.

The 369th also lost Lt John E Hughes (in P-51D-10 44-14188), who was last seen strafing a locomotive near Wittenberge. Listed as missing in action, his death was subsequently confirmed.

The final kill of this opening clash fell to the 369th's Lt Harold Burt when he shot the wing off an Fw 190, then joined up with Hatter of the 368th and headed home.

At 1200 hrs the 370th tangled with more enemy fighters some 20 miles south of Berlin. Lt Dick Connelly dived after a Bf 109 but was muscled out by an aggressive P-47 pilot who failed to score any hits and broke off at 6000 ft. Connelly then nailed the German fighter, which exploded upon hitting the ground. Low on fuel, he headed for base, and 20 minutes later he spotted a lone Fw 190 below him at 3000 ft. Connelly sent it exploding into the ground.

At 1250 hrs Red Flight, led by newly-crowned ace Lt Cyril Jones Jr, strafed an airfield south of Meindingen despite being ordered not to do so. Jones destroyed three single-engine aircraft, Lt John W Lamont claimed two and Lt Robert McInnes a Ju 52 and two single-engined aircraft, as well as damaging six others. Minutes later Jones paid the ultimate price for disobeying his seniors when he was shot down and killed while making another strafing pass. The wreckage of his fighter (P-51D-10 44-14071) was seen burning fiercely about 1000 yards from the airfield.

On the way home, Lt Eugene F Britton of the 368th ran out of fuel while making a landing approach at Abbeville, in France. The landing gear of his fighter was sheared off by camouflaged pits, and Britton spent the next three days hitching rides back to base. During an engagement near Berlin, the left aileron of Lt Robert Benefiel's P-51 was damaged when struck by the propeller of a Mustang from the 352nd. Benefiel flew home with the control stick pushed full right, and duly made a perfect wheels-up landing at the emergency airfield at Woodbridge, in Suffolk. Severe losses over the past 48 hours (seven Mustangs and five pilots on the 12th alone) led to an aircraft shortage, and Lt Col Swanson ordered all P-51s used for training to be made ready for combat.

On the 13th the 359th escorted B-24s attacking the synthetic oil industry at Merseburg once again. The group managed to sortie 44 P-51s, although 13 aborted. The increase in early returns was partly due to the use of war-weary training Mustangs, although it was amazing that the mechanics managed to get so many aircraft ready for service in the first place. The bombing results were excellent, but the B-24s failed to maintain formation, making it difficult for the fighters to escort assigned units. There were many stragglers, and the 359th stayed in the target area giving support to the last combat wings of bombers.

After a short break from long-range escort missions, the group returned to Germany on 25 September, when it looked after B-17s hitting industrial targets in Frankfurt. R/V was not made, so the 359th pressed on to the target area alone. At 1015 hrs, near Wiesbaden, Yellow Flight of the 368th met flak, and its pilots made an evasive turn, Lt John F Lauesen was seen going down in a vertical dive from 26,000 ft. One of eleven brothers, he had been hit by an 88 mm shell fired from a flak battery located near Hofheim. Witnesses at nearby Oberliederbach said that his P-51B had been trailing dark smoke, and when he bailed out his parachute had failed to open fully. The Mustang had been torn apart and ammunition was firing off when men from the gun crew arrived on the scene.

Lauesen's body was found about 200 yards from the wreckage, and two armed guards were posted nearby until it was collected the following morning. Although caskets were both scarce and expensive at this stage of the war, he was nevertheless buried in one. The Lauesen family lost two other sons during the war, one flying with the Navy and the other in the Marine Corps. Both flew Corsairs.

On 27 September the 359th supported B-17s bombing Düsseldorf. Only three Mustangs of the 51 taking off returned early. One of these was recent arrival Capt Fred S Hodges of the 369th, who was a former American Volunteer Group

Like Capt Ben King, Maj Fred S Hodges of the 369th FS had also fought the Japanese. In fact Hodges was a former 'Flying Tiger', having served with the American Volunteer Group's 3rd Pursuit Squadron in Burma and China in 1941-42 – he scored one kill against the Japanese. Forced to chase down the 359th after having initially aborted on 27 September 1944, Hodges' determination to complete the mission exemplified the mindset of the AVG. Assigned to Hodges, P-51D-10 *"JeePers"* (44-14313) was soon decorated with a shark's mouth on the nose to denote its pilot's service with the 'Flying Tigers'

'Flying Tiger' pilot with a solitary Japanese kill to his credit. Aborting soon after becoming airborne, Hodges landed, had the fault in his P-51 hastily repaired and then caught up with the group over the continent.

On 2 October Capt Benjamin King flew lead as the group escorted B-17s bombing Kassel, in Germany. R/V, at 0925 hrs, was over Brussels at 24,000 ft. Lt Donald E Cannon of the 369th turned back because of a dead radio, and soon the engine of his P-51 was running rough as well. He was over friendly territory in France when the engine finally ground to a halt and he bailed out safely. Cannon was back with his unit two days later after hitching a ride home in a B-24.

At 1110 hrs Blue Flight of the 370th dived to investigate reported bandits, but these turned out to be P-51s. While climbing back to resume their escort, they spotted five Bf 109s at 5000 ft. Diving from 20,000 ft proved futile, as by the time the Americans reached the area the enemy fighters had disappeared into low cloud. Blue Flight remained at low level, and as it approached Wabern, two trains were spotted. During the series of running attacks that stretched several miles, Lts Dick D Connelly, John W Lamont, Galen E Ramser and Lawrence Zizka destroyed 12 locomotives and 50 wagons.

Upon their return to East Wretham, acting group commander (Col Tacon was on leave) Lt Col Swanson made all four pilots sign a statement that they were aware of a current ban on opportunity strafing by Mustangs.

On 24 October the 359th flew the month's only authorised strafing mission, south-east of Hannover. Maj James K Lovett led, and the group arrived over the target area at 1430 hrs. Visibility was only one to three miles, but this did not stop the Mustang pilots from destroying 53 locomotives and damaging 95 wagons, along with 14 tanks that were being carried by the latter. Sixteen trucks were destroyed nearby, and more tanks damaged, and a much-hated flak gun and its five-man crew were also wiped out. Finally, a switch house was damaged and two flak towers destroyed.

At 1445 hrs Lt Merle Barth of the 368th, who was flying wing for Lt Paul E Olson, was pulling up from a strafing run on a truck when he lost sight of his colleague in the overcast. Barth then spotted an aircraft he assumed to be Olson's, and slid in close, before realising that it was an Fw 190. By the time the German was aware of his new wingman, Barth had slipped in behind him and fired two short bursts. The enemy pilot broke left and bailed out, while the fighter lost height and exploded.

At the same time the 368th's Flt Off Boyd N Adkins, who had become separated from his flight in the haze, had just pulled up from strafing a train when he spotted an aircraft he initially believed to be part of his flight. However, he soon recognised that it was another Fw 190, so he dropped his flaps, pulled in behind it and fired a three-second burst at close range. The Focke-Wulf pilot entered a left turn that ended in a terminal dive.

These two kills scored by the 368th were the only aerial victories for the nine Eighth Air Force fighter groups operating that day. The 53 locomotives destroyed by the 359th accounted for 39 per cent of the day's total for the nine groups. They also came across 'jack-in-the-box' barrage balloons for the first time. Carried on trains, these were designed to deploy to an altitude of 300 ft and provide protection against strafing fighters.

Lt Merle B Barth of the 368th FS poses in the cockpit of his P-51D-5 'CALIFORNIA COWBOY' (44-11159). His groundcrew are (from left to right) Sgt John Babola, S/Sgt Charles Doersom and S/Sgt Walter Wadley. Barth, who claimed two aerial victories, drowned in the English Channel on 20 November 1944 after he was forced to bail out of P-51D-10 44-14062 when it suffered mechanical failure

On 2 November the Group was back with the B-17s at Merseburg as the bombers hit the synthetic oil refineries again. The force arrived over the target at 1236 hrs, and as they exited less than ten minutes later, 30 Bf 109s attacked the bombers and shot down six of them. The 370th dived after the fleeing fighters and caught them at 12,000 ft. Capt Wetmore drew first blood, sending a Bf 109 into a terminal spin. Now alone, with only two functioning guns, he was set upon by 15-20 Messerschmitts. He fired a short burst, with about 70 degrees deflection, and using the new K-14 gunsight he hit his second victim in the cockpit. The German fighter stalled and tumbled to earth, while the remaining bandits scattered. This action earned Wetmore the Distinguished Service Cross, and boosted his tally to 10.25 kills – these were his first victories since 29 May.

Future five-kill ace Capt Ralph R Cox of the 369th claimed his first kill when he shot off one-third of the right wing of a Bf 109. Capt Sam J Huskins Jr also destroyed a Messerschmitt, which he shared with 343rd FS/55th FG pilot Lt Donald Mercier. Capt Dick D 'Dee Dee'

Lousy weather foiled operations against the enemy on 14 November 1944, but the 359th still managed some formation flying for the benefit of the camera. These two photos show a flight of P-51D-10s from the 370th FS, namely *Daddy's Girl* (CS-L/44-14733), flown by Capt Ray Wetmore, *RAYNER Shine* (CS-A/44-14521), flown by Lt Col Daniel McKee, *Mickey the Twist* (CS-G/44-14773), flown by Lt Emory Johnson, and *Blondie II* (CS-S/44-14192), flown by Capt Robert McInnes

Connelly claimed his third, and last aerial kill when the Bf 109 that he was attacking hit the ground and exploded before the pilot could bail out. Finally, at 1315 hrs, near Quedlinburg, Capt George Baker Jr and Lt Oscar R Faldmark of the 368th shared in the destruction of yet another Bf 109, the former also damaging a second Messerschmitt.

Maj James A Howard led an escort mission on the 5th for B-17s bombing the marshalling yards at Frankfurt, and this was followed up by a series of strafing attacks. The weather was so bad on this day that only the group's best 36 pilots were allowed to participate in this assignment. Two turned back before the rendezvous over Liege, in Belgium, at 1035 hrs, and visibility proved to be so poor over the target that the bombing had to be done by radar, with the escort finishing south-west of Koblenz at 1150 hrs. Just after parting company with the 'Forts', the 368th was forced to split up after running into intense flak. The bad weather meant that the pilots could not regroup, so White Flight escorted some crippled B-17s out while Blue Flight strafed and destroyed two locomotives and five trucks.

The 369th also attacked some trains, and the unit's Lt Maurice M Haines had his Mustang (P-51D-15 44-14857) struck by ground fire whilst strafing a locomotive near Wendelsheim. He crash-landed near

Darmstadt and was taken prisoner. Other claims for the day included 12 locomotives destroyed and 41 wagons damaged, as well as six trucks destroyed. The Americans also wrecked a bus loaded with troops. The 12 locomotives accounted for a third of those destroyed by VIII Fighter Command that day, with all 15 groups seeing action.

Col Tacon led the 359th for the last time on 9 November as it headed for Metz, supporting B-17s attacking transport targets. Three days later Lt Col John P Randolph from the 20th FG assumed command of the 359th as Col Tacon became chief of staff to Brig Gen Edward W Anderson, CO of the 67th FW.

On 21 November Maj Roy W Evans led the 359th as it once again looked after B-17s bombing synthetic oil targets at Merseburg. The group put up 59 fighters at 0917 hrs, four of which dropped out. The first action occurred west of the target at 1135 hrs. The leader of the 369th's Green Flight, Lt Claude J Crenshaw, and his wingman, Lt Harold Tenenbaum, were alone (Green 3 and 4 aborted due to poor visibility) when a bandit warning came over the radio. Flying at 31,000 ft, Crenshaw spotted about 100 Fw 190s, with a top cover of about 35 more, trailing above a formation of bombers. They dropped down behind the bandits and saw eight P-51s from the 352nd FG closing in on the German fighters.

These P-51Ds from the 369th FS (top) and a mix of B- and D-models from the 369th and 370th (bottom) were also seen on the 14th. The trio of P-51Ds are *Precious Pat* (IV-P/ 44-14543), flown by Capt Gilbert R Ralston, IV-Z (44-15007), flown by Lt Thomas J Klem, and IV-D (44-15394), of Rene Burtner. In the bottom photo are P-51Ds *X-Terminator* (IV-X/ 44-14218), CS-C (44-14096), CS-V (44-14096) and IV-T (44-15081), P-51C IV-G (42-103793) and P-51B IV-H (42-106476). Note that the latter two have had dorsal strakes added

Crenshaw lined up on an Fw 190, but a 352nd P-51 cut in, forcing him to pick another target. After a second burst of fire, a Focke-Wulf rolled over and the pilot bailed out. Victim number two was hit with a short burst from 75 yards, and this pilot also bailed out. Popping out of the haze, Crenshaw then found 50 more Fw 190s firing on the bombers. He slipped behind one of the attackers and fired two short bursts into its engine. The Fw 190 rolled over, fire trailing from its nose and went down. Climbing back through the haze, Crenshaw engaged about 30 bandits and scored hits on one in the cockpit area. He was then forced to break off as two Germans latched on to his tail and started firing at him.

After clearing 'his six', Crenshaw jumped two more bandits and they dived for the deck. As he fired on one of them, the other fighter got behind

A veteran of the Pacific Theatre, as well as a tour with the 20th FG's HQ flight, Lt Col John P Randolph assumed command of the 359th in November 1944, and remained in charge until April 1945. He had scored one aerial and four strafing victories during the course of his 26 missions with the 20th FG (flown between July and November 1944), and he had these marked on the canopy rail of his assigned Mustang, P-51D-15 44-14965. This aircraft lost its invasion stripes in early 1945, and simultaneously had its name changed to *LADY*

him, which in turn allowed a Mustang from the 352nd FG to shoot it down. Crenshaw then watched as his prey dived into the ground at 600 mph. Once back at base, it was discovered that only three of his six guns had been working due to ammunition jams. Crenshaw, who had boosted his finally tally to seven aerial and three ground strafing kills following his quartet of victories during this mission, attributed his latest success to the K-14 gunsight and recently-introduced G-Suit (the latter prevented him from blacking out during aggressive combat manoeuvring at high speed).

Tenenbaum, meanwhile, had engaged an Fw 190 on Crenshaw's tail at the start of the fight, and scored hits in both the wing roots. The German jettisoned his canopy, but Tenenbaum continued firing until the fighter pushed over into a descending spiral, its pilot apparently dead.

At 1145 hrs Lt Carl M Anderson reported that his Merlin (in P-51D-10 44-14444) was losing oil pressure and vibrating. The engine duly caught fire, forcing him to belly-land his fighter in a muddy field near Sonderhausen, where he was taken prisoner. As for the bombers, they hit their target with the help of radar just before 1200 hrs, despite heavy flak.

Minutes later the 370th engaged a large numbers of enemy fighters halfway between Kassel and the target. Capt William Hodges, who was leading Red Flight at 31,000 ft, spotted about 50 Fw 190s some 2000 ft below, flying west. He led the bounce, pulling in behind the enemy formation. His first burst damaged the trailing German fighter just as the rest of the formation dipped into haze. Hodges followed blindly, then climbed out of the mist to find that the Germans had done the same.

His first kill was achieved at a range of just 300 yards, with the Fw 190 left smoking before it entered a high-speed spin. The rest of the formation was still unaware of the presence of the Americans as Hodges pulled in

P-51D-15 *HEAT WAVE* (44-15016) was just one of three Mustangs that seven-kill ace Capt Crenshaw was assigned during his seven-month tour with the 369th. He claimed a quartet of Fw 190s in this machine on 21 November 1944 to 'make ace'

Hailing from Monroe, Louisiana, Capt Crenshaw also scored three ground strafing kills as well as seven aerial victories. He completed his tour with 270 combat hours

Lt Col Daniel McKee commanded the 370th FS from 11 September 1944 until 21 April 1945, and he finished his tour with one kill in the air and four on the ground. He is seen here posing with his P-51D-10 *RAYNER Shine* (44-14521). McKee's last assigned Mustang was P-51D-25 *RAYNER Shine* (44-72823), which was passed on to the Swiss Air Force post-war

behind two more bandits flying a tight wing, and his first burst hit one in the canopy. As he hammered the Fw 190 again, it made a slight left turn while the fighter on the left moved to the right. Holding down the trigger, Hodges riddled both fighters, with one going down in a spin and the other in flames.

White Flight now joined the battle, and their leader, Maj McKee, fired on a Fw 190 just as another P-51 cut in, blocking his aim. McKee slid over behind a second Fw 190, fired a short burst but saw no hits. Picking out a third enemy fighter, he did get some strikes this time, and continued firing until the Focke-Wulf began to burn.

At around the same time, Lt Thomas Smith blasted some large pieces off an Fw 190, causing it to snap down to the right for kill number one. As his first victim was going down, another Focke-Wulf slid in front of him from the right – a four-second burst tore off sections of the fighter, these flying back past Smith's P-51. The bandit also snapped down to the right, becoming kill number two. The Mustang pilot then banked right and fired at an Fw 190 from 200 yards. This one was hit in the left wing root and was later credited to Smith as a probable. Levelling out, he pulled in behind a fourth Focke-Wulf and proceeded to score hits in its left wing root. The enemy fighter rolled over to the right and down, and was also awarded as a probable. Smith recalled;

'Ray Wetmore was flying close escort down below, and he knew something was going on because he started yelling his fool head off, "Send down a live one, send down a live one!" He was down below calling, "Where are they?" I said "They're up here. They're coming down, they're coming down". He said, "all that's coming down are burning aeroplanes and parachutes. To hell with that, send me a live one"!'

Lt Vernon L Caid, also of White Flight, pulled in behind the enemy formation, damaging his first target before having to break off. Moving back into firing position Caid scored hits in the cockpit of a second fighter and the pilot bailed out. He chased his next victim in a dive, hitting it with several long bursts, before pulling out at 4000 ft while the Fw 190 went down at almost 600 mph.

However, the fight was not one-sided, for the pilots of the 370th witnessed six B-17s being shot down from which only one parachute was seen. The 370th also lost Lt Stanley F Stegnerski (in P-51D-10 44-14185), who was killed by German fighters.

Blue Flight of the 370th, was one of the last to enter the fray, and its leader, Capt Will D Burgsteiner, scored hits on an Fw 190 just as the three guns in his left wing jammed. Diving away, the enemy fighter was hit in the left wing, across the fuselage and into the right wing for a probable kill. Burgsteiner then climbed back into the battle and fired several bursts at another Fw 190 but saw no strikes. Lt John W Lamont damaged a third Focke-Wulf before losing it in the haze.

Black Flight's Lt Homer A Staup fired on a fighter from 'six o'clock', and noted strikes on both it and the Fw 190 directly ahead of his intended target! Closing to within 100 yards, Staup fired again and the nearest Focke-Wulf exploded, while the second Fw 190 pulled up in a chandelle and the pilot bailed out.

Future five-kill ace Capt Ralph L 'Slick' Cox, the leader and last remaining pilot from Black Flight, then took on some 50 enemy fighters.

Singling out one on the left flank, he fired two long bursts from 45 degrees and scored a few hits before the pilot bailed out. Now at 20,000 ft, Cox spotted another formation of 50 enemy fighters attacking the bombers. As he levelled out of his climb at 35,000 ft, he could see three more gaggles of about 50 Fw 190s. Cox continued his ascent to 40,000 ft, screaming for help over his radio.

Ten minutes later, as he positioned himself to bounce the last group of fighters, he spotted six P-51s climbing up towards him. Cox went into a dive, swooped down in front of the approaching Mustangs and called over his radio for them to follow. Thinking he was covered, he singled out an Fw 190 and fired two bursts from dead astern. The pilot bailed out.

Pulling in behind victim number two, Cox hammered it until it exploded. Tracers then burned past his P-51, and he found he had eight bandits on his 'six'. He pulled away in a climbing spiral and headed home, still very much alone. Cox later reported having seen about 250 enemy fighters – none of them seemed to have wanted a fight, except for the eight that latched on to his tail. This was perhaps due to the fact that many Fw 190 pilots pressed into service at this late stage of the war had been pulled from ground attack units, and were not well trained in air combat.

At 1230 hrs, near Erfurt, Yellow Flight of the 368th spotted about 100 Fw 190s 5000 ft below them, parallel to and beneath the bombers. As they bounced the bandits, Lt John Keesey picked out a target and fired off a burst. There was a flash and a puff of smoke just prior to the fighter commencing a turn. Keesey followed the damaged machine down, and pulled the trigger several times, but all six of his guns were jammed. On returning to England, it was found that only three guns had fired. Keesey was credited with one enemy fighter damaged.

Whilst this was taking place, another flight from the 368th, led by Capt Thomas McGeever, was nearing Gotha in search of an airfield to strafe. Lt Emory Cook spotted a well camouflaged Fw 190 base, and as the flight made a pass, they encountered the heaviest ground fire many of them had ever experienced. McGeever destroyed an Fw 190, but the coolant system in his Mustang (P-51D-10 44-14670) was hit and he radioed that he was bailing out. He was later reported killed in action.

The mission on 27 November was a scheduled strafing operation against an airfield at Ehmen, in Germany. However, before the Americans reached Dummer Lake, bandits were reported north of Münster, and most of the group dropped their tanks to divert and investigate. The pilots met heavy flak on the way, and the 359th broke into flights to evade the barrage. The 'bandits' turned out to be Mustangs, and the 359th was now scattered, with some flights having to head home because of limited fuel.

Red Flight of the 370th, led by Capt Wetmore, was making for Ehmen when he spotted two formations of fighters south-east of Hannover. One consisted of about 100 Bf 109s and the other a similar number of Fw 190s. Wetmore contacted the remnants of the group, giving his position and altitude. Minutes later Capt Robert McInnes (Red 4), reported engine trouble, and Wetmore ordered Lt Jimmy Shoffit to escort him back to base.

Three minutes later, as Wetmore and his wingman, future five-kill ace Lt Robert 'Rudy' York, were shadowing the rear group of Bf 109s at 'six o'clock high', they were discovered, and several four-ship flights turned to engage them. With no help in sight, and trouble on the way, Wetmore and

27 November 1944 was a memorable day for future five-kill ace Lt Robert Miles 'Rudy' York of the 370th FS. While he and Ray Wetmore were shadowing 200 enemy fighters near Lüneburg, anxiously waiting for reinforcements to arrive, they were spotted by the German formation. Wetmore told York, 'You take the hundred on the right and I'll take the hundred on the left'! When the smoke cleared, both Wetmore and York had destroyed three Bf 109s apiece, with the latter also being credited with a fourth as a probable. York 'made ace' on New Year's Day 1945

York attacked despite odds of 100-to-1. Scoring his first kill at 600 yards, Wetmore used his K-14 gunsight to deadly effect, sending a Bf 109 spinning down in flames. York followed up, sending another Messerschmitt earthward billowing black smoke. Wetmore then scored hits on a second Bf 109 from 300 yards at 20 degrees deflection, before sending a third fighter tumbling down trailing smoke. As yet another fighter attacked, Wetmore banked into his opponent and the pair dived from 30,000 ft to the deck, with the advantage switching back and forth. Wetmore scored several hits before running out of ammunition, but the enemy pilot bailed out nevertheless when the ace manoeuvred back into a firing position.

This engagement had lasted 25 minutes, and Wetmore's P-51D-15 (44-14979) had taken two 20 mm hits in the left gun bay. For the next ten minutes he was repeatedly attacked by Fw 190s, but he managed to outmanoeuvre them until they broke off. Wetmore then headed back to base.

York, meanwhile, had been pressing home his attacks, sliding in behind a Bf 109 and scoring numerous hits until the enemy fighter tumbled out of control, shedding parts and smoking. Suddenly, another Bf 109 passed about 800 yards in front of him in a slight dive. Closing in, York employed his K-14 gunsight to deliver a long-range shot, and the fighter exploded.

He then spotted a Bf 109 turning into him from slightly above. Cutting the German off in the turn, York began firing at 500 yards, holding his trigger down until he pulled up and over the Bf 109. Just then he noticed tracers passing over his wing, so he hastily pulled into a quarter snap and spin manoeuvre in order to evade his attacker. York almost collided with the Bf 109 that he had just shot up, and he got a close-up view of the pilot in the process of bailing out. Diving past the pilotless fighter, York picked up speed in a spiral to keep his tail clear, levelled off in a cloud layer and headed home.

By now Blue Flight of the 370th had joined in the fight, diving on a formation of Bf 109s from 34,000 ft. Levelling out at 28,000 ft, Lt Dick Connelly (Blue 3) and his wingman, Lt Donald L 'Windy' Windmiller, (Blue 4) pulled in behind the German fighters, and the latter pilot nailed a Bf 109 from 500 yards, sending it down in flames.

Looking back to clear his 'six', 'Windy' noticed a bandit moving into a firing position. He pulled the Mustang up in a sharp 180-degree turn that he knew the Bf 109 pilot could not match – it duly stalled and dropped its nose. 'Windy' then saw another Messerschmitt closing on him from 90 degrees. He turned to meet the attacker, got on his tail and fired a long burst from 500 yards, scoring a few hits. Closing to just 300 yards Windmiller fired again and the Bf 109 nosed over in flames. Whilst in the process of scoring his second kill, 'Windy' received a radio call from Dick Connelly, who said 'The son of a bitch has shot me down, "Windy". I'm bailing out.' Connelly (flying P-51D-10 44-14096) had

Capt Dick Connelly and the P-51D-10 in which he would lose his life on 27 November 1944. Rushing to the aid of Wetmore and York, Connelly, in *De De III* (44-14096), led Blue Flight of the 370th FS into the thick of the action north of Kassel, and was shot down minutes later. His premonition that he would be killed on the last mission of his tour sadly proved to be correct. Dick Connelly, who had been in the ETO since May 1944, had three aerial victories to his credit by the time of his demise

had a premonition that he would die on the last mission of his tour, and it came true. Alone and low on fuel, 'Windy' headed for England.

Headquarters pilot Maj Roy Evans was leading a flight from the 369th FS that responded to Wetmore's call for help. He was joined by Maj Niven Cranfill and his wingman, Lt Richard H Daniels, of the 368th. At 1305 hrs these six Mustangs arrived on the scene at 31,000 ft.

They made a diving attack from out of the sun on the rear of the enemy formation, Evans firing a burst from 50 degrees that took

more than a foot off a Bf 109's wing, but he then broke off when a second fighter latched onto his tail. Moving back into a firing position, he took aim at another Bf 109 at an angle of 30-35 degrees from 250 yards, closing to 200 yards, and saw the left side of the fighter's engine and fuselage being struck. This fighter turned left, rolled over and spun down on fire. Evans was credited with one damaged and one destroyed. These were his last claims of the war, the former RAF 'Eagle' Squadron pilot having joined the 359th FG in October following a successful tour with the 335th FS/4th FG. He had claimed four aerial kills with the 335th (which he had led for a time in 1943-44) to add to his solitary RAF victory.

The 369th's Lt Robert T Lancaster also scored a victory in this clash when a Bf 109 crossed in front and below him. Firing from 70 degrees, he hit the enemy's wing roots and fuselage near the cockpit. The fighter began to smoke, snapping into a spin. Maj Cranfill, meanwhile, had fired on a Bf 109 during a sharp evasive action, but he could not see any hits. He followed the German down in a vertical dive, and the Bf 109's canopy came off. The fighter then zoomed up in a sharp climb and the pilot jumped clear, sailing past Cranfill before opening his parachute. The

A true veteran of the ETO, Lt Col Roy Evans flew 15 missions in the RAF with No 121 'Eagle' Sqn in 1942 before joining the newly-formed 4th FG when it absorbed the trio of American-manned RAF fighter units in September of that year. He scored five aerial kills whilst flying with the 4th FG's 335th FS, and added a sixth victory (plus a strafing kill) following his transfer to the 359th's HQ flight in August 1944. Evans was shot down by flak on 14 February 1945 whilst flying P-51D-15 44-14894. Badly wounded, he spent the rest of the war in a German hospital (*Cook*)

A two-tour veteran with the 359th FG, Maj Niven Cranfill served as the 369th's Ops Officer during his first spell in the ETO, which lasted from October 1943 through to July 1944. Returning to the group as CO of the 368th FS three months later, Cranfill scored three aerial kills (two Bf 109s and an Fw 190) on 27 November 1944, which earned him a second Silver Star. He is seen here with his groundcrew, (from left to right) armourer Sgt Anthony Chardella, assistant crew chief Cpl Tony Castellano and crew chief S/Sgt Ernest Behn. Chardella applied the painting on Cranfill's P-51D-5 *DEVILESS 3* (44-13390). 'Cranny' completed 133 missions totalling 506 combat hours, and scored five aerial kills, one shared probable kill and two damaged. Post-war, he remained in the Air Force, serving both in Korea and Vietnam, before retiring in January 1970

These two photos show the routine task of filling up the Mustang's capacious wing and fuselage fuel tanks. The aircraft being 'tanked up' is the 368th's P-51D-5 *"COOKIE "* (44-13762), and the fellows doing the filling are (left) S/Sgt Ira J Bisher, with a little help from fuel truck operator Cpl John E Conklin, and (above) S/Sgt Kenneth S Wilson. The fuselage tank was used early in the mission to eliminate the tail-heavy condition it created when full. Indeed, at least two pilots in the group were lost when they entered combat with too much fuel remaining in their fuselage tank. Note the mud on the ventral scoop. Mud would also get inside the scoop, clogging the radiator core. This could easily cause engine overheating, and the problem was eventually remedied by converting an old fuel truck into a water-carrying decontaminator unit. Spraying water directly into the scoop eliminated a potential abort from a 'popped' coolant plug. This particular Mustang saw a lot of combat, being flown regularly by Howard Fogg and John Gordon. Fogg initially christened it *"MOOSE NOSE"*, although it was later renamed *"COOKIE"*. This aircraft had the dubious distinction of being involved in the 359th's last fatal crash in the ETO on 23 July 1945. Flt Off John Klug Jr had just departed East Wretham when he felt a loss of power. Turning back towards his Norfolk base, Klug soon realised he would not make it home and chose instead to make a forced landing in a field. However, the fighter suddenly snapped inverted and crashed, killing Klug outright (*Bisher*)

Major was then at 8000 ft, and seven minutes had elapsed since the fight had begun.

Latching on to an Fw 190, he chased it over a small town, where his Mustang drew some ground fire. Looking back to clear his tail, Cranfill found a P-51 from the 357th FG following him, and he was grateful for the cover. Cranfill's windscreen had iced over in his high-speed dive, and he only succeeded in partially clearing it with his glove. Despite this handicap, he managed to keep the Fw 190 in his sights and fire several effective bursts. However, due to a haze, and the slate grey camouflage of his opponent, Cranfill lost his prey. However, Flt Off Thomas W Jackson, who was covering Cranfill, saw the Fw 190 crash and confirmed it as a kill.

Now below 500 ft, the Major spotted a Bf 109 crossing above him from left to right, and he quickly pulled in behind it. The warmer air at low altitude was rapidly melting the ice off the windscreen of his P-51, thus making it easier for Cranfill to stay with the German fighter. Both aircraft had their flaps in combat position, but the American was able to turn inside the Bf 109 and hit it several times from about 300 yards. Finally the Messerschmitt pulled up, stalled, dived straight into the ground and exploded. Jackson was still there, and confirmed Cranfill's third kill. It was later found that only two of his guns were functioning, and only 588 rounds had been fired.

The 368th's Lt Richard H Daniels had engaged an Fw 190 during the initial bounce, scoring hits in the fuselage near the canopy. The pilot of the German fighter then rolled it over and headed for the deck, kicking his fighter from side to side to make it hard to hit. In the haze, Daniels lost the Focke-Wulf, which was trailing black smoke. On returning to base it was discovered that only his left outboard gun had fired, and that a mere 65 rounds of armour-piercing incendiary had been used up. Daniel's claim of an Fw 190 destroyed was later amended to a probable.

On 12 December the 359th laid on an escort for B-17s heading back to Merseburg, Lt Col John Randolph leading 'A' group and Lt Col McKee being put in charge of 'B' group. The bombing was a success, and only one B-17 was lost. Over the radio the Mustang pilots heard that RAF Lancasters were being attacked near Dortman, and the 370th duly went to their rescue. They chased off about 30 Bf 109s, but not before five Lancasters had been shot down. While giving chase, the squadron was jumped by an even larger force of fighters flying top cover. The whole enemy force was then lost in the clouds, and the 370th returned to base without having fired a shot.

On the 13th M/Sgt Arthur E Newman and T/Sgt Lawrence F Haas of the 368th FS were each awarded the Bronze Star for inventions that increased the operational efficiency of the group. Newman had designed and built an engine pre-oiler that increased the life of the Merlin engine by three hours. His contribution to increased maintenance efficiency and an 87 per cent better service rate for the 368th's aircraft were also cited.

Haas designed new sway braces for drop tanks after the factory-supplied units began breaking and puncturing the tanks. These braces were manufactured by the group's service squadron, and they were adopted by all of VIII Fighter Command's groups. Haas also designed pressurisation fittings for drop tanks, and by the end of December 1944 these fittings had been used on about 8100 drop tanks without one failure.

The 368th FS had two pilots make 'ace-in-a-day' on 18 December 1944, namely Lts David B Archibald (below) and Paul Olson (bottom). Having both claimed five Fw 190s apiece, the pair were brought down by flak, and the severe injuries Archibald sustained when his P-51 crashed plagued him for the rest of his life – he passed away in February 1998

Haas also modified a fuel trailer into an ethylene glycol dispenser, making it possible to quickly service the entire squadron, and thus eliminate waste.

On 17 December the pilots were finally told about the mysterious 'Big Ben' contrails they had spotted high in the continental sky since October. They were caused by German V2 ballistic rockets fired in the direction of southern England, against which there was no defence.

The following day was another red-letter occasion for the 359th, as two pilots from the 368th FS – Lts David Archibald and Paul Olson – each became 'aces in a day', which was a feat equalled only once in the history of the Eighth Air Force. The group provided penetration, target and withdrawal support for B-17s raiding the marshalling yards at Cologne, and of the 53 Mustangs sortied from East Wretham, only one turned back. Rendezvous with the bombers was over Hannut, in Belgium, but the weather was so bad that more than 500 of the 985 bombers scheduled to participate in the mission had to return home. The 'Forts' that were escorted by the 359th looked for targets of opportunity, but after 20 minutes they turned back without dropping their loads. The 359th was told to stay with the remaining bombers.

At 1300 hrs, and at 32,000 ft, Lt Olson was hampered by freezing ailerons and, escorted by Lt Archibald, he dropped down to 10,000 ft so that his controls would thaw out. At 1340 hrs a radio message was received that 60+ bandits had been detected between Kassel and Cologne, although the 359th was told to stay with its charges. Archibald and Olson headed in the direction of Cologne to investigate the report, and soon noticed a B-17 that had apparently crash-landed. Archibald radioed to Olson that he would drop his fuel tanks on the bomber, and he told him to strafe the 'Fort' and set it on fire. As they approached the B-17 someone was seen getting out of it, so they broke off their attack.

As Archibald circled for another look, camouflaged 20 mm flak guns opened up, and he was hit in the left thigh by a shell fragment – the pain was dulled because his legs were still cold from the time spent at 32,000 ft. Five minutes later he and Olson spotted the enemy fighters, and approaching them from the rear, they used the element of surprise and attacked. Engaging the formation of Fw 190s from an angle of 30 degrees, Archibald quickly shot down two and Olson one. Strangely, the formation didn't break, so they swung around for another pass. This time they overshot the last flight, and Archibald bagged the leader of the next flight while Olson downed the leader's wingman.

Now the Fw 190s split up in confusion, and during his third pass Archibald destroyed another bandit, while Olson registered some good hits on his intended victim, and noticed the pilot bail out. The empty Fw 190 collided with another, and they both exploded. Manoeuvring for a fourth strike, Olson saw flak burst behind them, but continued the attack.

Two Fw 190s then attempted to intercept the Mustangs from the left and right, only to collide head-on and become victims nine and ten. Archibald fired more rounds into the fuselage of another Fw 190, but the flak gunners had their range and both P-51s were struck. Olson's fighter (P-51D-10 44-14131) exploded, and he was thrown clear covered in flaming fuel and oil. He beat out the flames in time to pull the rip cord, and his parachute opened.

Captured by a flak guncrew at Vohn, he was taken to a doctor then driven by ambulance to a frontline hospital at Hoffmonstahl.

Archibald, meanwhile, had passed out from loss of blood following the earlier shrapnel wound, and his battle-damaged Mustang (P-51D-15 44-15555) crashed and exploded. Hurled 100 ft from the wreckage on impact, amazingly Archibald was found unconscious seven hours later – and he was put on the same ambulance carrying Olson! Interned in Hoffmonstahl hospital for two weeks, during which time he enjoyed just brief moments of consciousness, Archibald remembered someone mentioning Christmas, then Happy New Year. When he next came round he was shocked to find himself a PoW.

He passed out again, and not surprisingly – the pain he had had to endure was caused by a spine fractured in five places, eight broken ribs, a broken left shoulder blade, right wrist and two bones in the right hand, as well as a fractured skull. The next time he woke up, an air raid was in progress, and a hot piece of shrapnel hurtled through an open window and hit his bad leg. Archibald was moved to a room where Olson was in the next bed, and within days both of them, along with 220 other Allied airmen, were packed into railway wagons and taken to *Stalag 11B* in Fallingbostel. The camp was liberated on 16 April, and Archibald hobbled to freedom on two sticks, with years of medical treatment ahead of him.

Maj Roy Evans led 'A' group and Lt Col McKee 'B' group on 23 December when the 359th escorted B-17s sent to bomb a railway junction and marshalling yards at Homburg, in Germany. Rendezvous was north of the German town of Trier at 1220 hrs, and five minutes later the 368th's White Flight heard over the radio that bandits had been spotted climbing near Koblenz.

As they headed off to intercept the enemy, the pilots saw a straggling B-17 being attacked by a Bf 109. Lt Robert E Benefiel (White 1) turned to attack, and a second Messerschmitt appeared from behind his flight and was tackled by Lt Emory Cook. The latter quickly forced his opponent to bail out. In the meantime, Benefiel followed his target through a series of manoeuvres before getting in a good burst that sent the Bf 109 and its pilot down in a smoking, terminal, vertical dive. Later on, a 368th flight, led by Capt Wilbur Lewis, spotted a jet fighter – erroneously identified as an 'He 280', this aircraft was almost certainly an Me 262 – but the Americans could not get near it.

The Eighth Air Force's biggest mission of the war, at least in terms of the number of aircraft involved, was flown on 24 December, some 2046 heavy bombers and 853 fighters being sortied. The 359th also set a record when it sent off 76 Mustangs, only four of which aborted. Split up into 'A' and 'B' groups, the 359th looked after B-17s raiding airfields in Germany.

At 1345 hrs, near Vogelsand, Yellow Flight of the 369th, led by Lt John E Keur, was told of a Bf 109 approaching the bomber stream. When intercepted, the German went into a dive, pulling out at 18,000 ft. Keur fired two bursts and saw his rounds hit the fuselage before he overshot his prey. Getting back on its tail, he then chased the enemy fighter in another dive, scoring more strikes before his guns jammed.

At this point Keur called on his wingman, Lt Bryce H Thomson, to take over the attack. The Bf 109 succeeded in climbing back to 15,000 ft before it was caught by Thomson, who fired a five-second burst into its cockpit and engine. The fighter duly burst into flames and crashed with the pilot still aboard.

This proved to be a portent of things to come, for Bryce Thomson's P-51 also caught fire (due to mechanical problems) as he headed back to base, but unlike his German foe, he managed to bail out near Dinant, in Belgium. Luckily for him, his parachute carried him to the west bank of the Meuse river, and into friendly territory.

Meanwhile, Lt John J Kelly III (Yellow 3) had spotted another Bf 109 starting to attack a straggling 'Fort'. Firing a long burst from 30 down to 0 degrees deflection, he hit the Messerschmitt's right wing, tail and fuselage. The bandit rolled over and went down trailing white smoke, then tumbled out of control into a forest and exploded.

Good bombing results were reported by the 370th on an airfield at Giessen, in Germany, where enemy aircraft were seen exploding. The 369th reported good hits on an airfield at Hattenrod too, and several other targets in the area. On the way home, the 359th was vectored from northeast of Giessen to Bonn, and at 1520 hrs the 368th and 370th intercepted enemy fighters at 20,000 ft over Cologne.

There were two formations of bandits, one consisting of 12+ Fw 190s and the other of between 15 and 20 Bf 109s. About 15 miles to the south, some 100 Ninth Air Force B-26 Marauders were also spotted, and these were probably the intended target of the enemy fighters. Black Flight of the 368th, led by Lt Elby Beal, jumped the Fw 190s. The leader engaged four Fw 190s, only to discover that his guns would not fire. Soon they were spluttering erratically, and Beal sent two of the fighters down on Cologne. A Bf 109 then latched onto his tail, and while firing almost rammed him. As the German flew by, Beal tried to get a shot at him, but an Fw 190 got between them. Beal fired several bursts from 25 yards, dead astern of the hapless Focke-Wulf, and pieces flew off the fighter which began trailing smoke. It then entered a steep dive, its pilot probably dead.

Lt Ray A Boyd (Black 3) also got behind an Fw 190, hitting its left wing and fuselage. Intent on his kill, he failed to notice that another Fw 190 had slipped behind him. Boyd's Mustang (P-51D-10 44-14329) was badly hit, wounding the pilot in the left leg and foot. Lt Leonard Carter tried and failed to raise him on the radio, and it was later learned that Boyd had bailed out and been taken prisoner.

The 370th's Lt John Wilson joined the fight just in time to see Boyd being shot down. Cutting out four chequered-nose Mustangs chasing the victorious Fw 190, Wilson gave it a long burst from 150 yards with 70-80 degrees deflection. The Fw 190 burst into flames and the canopy popped off, but the pilot did not bail out. The doomed fighter entered a slow downward spin.

Capt Andrew Lemmens credited his K-14 gunsight with an incredible 800-yard shot during this action, his rounds hitting an Fw 190 in the cockpit with such force that it caused an explosion that sent flames shooting out across both wings. The Fw 190 entered a 75-degree dive and exploded when it hit the ground. Wilson then joined Lemmens and headed home.

Lt Robert G Oakley followed an Fw 190 from 10,000 ft in a dive that reached more than 500 mph, watching brown smoke trail from the fighter as he fired rounds into it. Both machines then started to pull out of the

dive, but only Oakley succeeded – the Fw 190 ploughed into the ground and exploded.

Lt Emory G Johnson (White 2) hit an Fw 190 in the wing, but was then forced to break when a second Focke-Wulf got in behind him. Shaking off the German fighter, Johnson latched onto yet another Fw 190. His foe was damaged around the canopy, and dived straight into the ground. Banking to the right, Johnson fired on another Fw 190, hitting its right wing. His second kill came when he bounced a fourth Focke-Wulf at 2000 ft, firing a burst into its fuselage aft of the cockpit which caused an explosion that threw the fighter into a spin.

The last kill for Christmas Eve fell to Capt William Hodges (White 3), who enjoyed an early Christmas present when he 'made ace' by sending an Fw 190 down in flames following a stern attack.

On the 31st the 359th was once again split into 'A' and 'B' groups, and they escorted B-17s that were heading for a German oil refinery at Misburg and an aircraft factory, with an adjacent airfield, at Wenzendorf. Rendezvous was over the German island of Langeoog at 1040 hrs. Just over an hour later, north-west of Hamburg, Lt William F Collins, leader of the 369th's Blue Flight, and his wingman, Lt Arthur B Morris, were flying above the bomber stream at 27,000 ft when two Me 262s were spotted approaching from 'six o'clock level'. Collins and Morris turned right and got in fleeting shots at the passing jets.

Morris then saw one of them shoot down a P-51 before they passed out of range. The pair then chased an Fw 190 that was attacking the bombers, and the gunners on the 'Forts' bagged it. Minutes later two more jets were seen approaching the bombers, and once more the Mustangs drove them away. As the Me 262s left, four Fw 190s flew past the Mustangs, and Collins broke after them. Morris saw 15 Focke-Wulf fighters diving for the deck, and as they pursued them one went into a spin and crashed. Collins and Morris shared in the destruction of two more, from which the pilots bailed out.

At 1150 hrs, Red, White and Blue Flights of the 370th were passing over Hannover at 32,000 ft, on their way to the second rendezvous, when ten or more Bf 109s were spotted at '12 o'clock low' (31,000 ft). The 370th bounced the bandits, and Lt Frank O Lux got into a tight turn with

This A-20 Havoc, belonging to the 3rd Gunnery and Tow-Target Flight, was used to take operations personnel from East Wretham to Reims, in France, to fly the 27 December 1944 mission that was staged from there by 'C' group. When it returned two days later, the Havoc brought with it 50 bottles of 1937 vintage champagne, which added greatly to the festive cheer of the Christmas season. The Havoc was badly damaged in an apparent crash-landing at East Wretham in April 1945, photos taken at the time revealing that its nose gear had collapsed

The 370th's Lt Galen E Ramser poses with his groundcrew in front of their P-51D-5 *Zombie II* (44-13604). This aircraft was a replacement for his much-loved P-51B-15 *Zombie* (43-24778), which was destroyed on 30 September 1944 when its engine faltered on take-off. *Zombie II* sustained major damage on 10 December 1944 when the right main gear leg collapsed during take-off. While he never scored an aerial kill, Ramser was nevertheless in the thick of the action, helping to destroy 18 locomotives. He completed his tour in March 1945

one of the German pilots, scoring numerous hits that set his fighter ablaze. The Bf 109 went into a spin and the pilot failed to escape. Lux then latched onto the tail of another Messerschmitt and scored three hits.

Lt Lawrence A Zizka also downed a Bf 109, puncturing its drop tank and enveloping it in flames. The blazing fighter dived straight into the ground. Meanwhile, Lux's wingman, Lt Emory Johnson, took on two Bf 109s, and he and a Mustang pilot from the 4th FG shared in destroying one, which burst into flames and spun down. Lt Jack E McCoskey then drove off a Bf 109 that was attacking Lux, hitting it twice before two Mustangs and two Thunderbolts cut him out of the action. McCoskey then returned to base.

Capt Wetmore also hit a Bf 109, sending it spinning down trailing smoke with his third burst. His second victim was caught at treetop height over Hannover, and the fighter was hit from astern at between 300 and 500 yards. As the German bellied in, Lt Werner J Rueschenberg hit him again, causing the Bf 109 to disintegrate as it cartwheeled to a stop.

Capt Lemmens riddled another Bf 109, starting a fire in the cockpit, and he followed it down for 10,000 ft before breaking off. Lt Galen Ramser bounced a Messerschmitt and fired bursts from 300 yards at 20 degrees deflection in a turn, hitting the left wing and fuselage. He then followed the damaged fighter in a dive, seeing strikes near the cockpit as they levelled out at 6000 ft. Again he hit the Bf 109, this time from only 50 ft dead astern. Its engine started smoking and the pilot lowered his gear – a sign of surrender. Out of ammunition, Ramser broke off his attack.

At 1215 hrs, south-east of Stade, in Germany, Capt George Baker Jr was leading the 368th's Blue Flight when eight Fw 190s sliced head-on through the bombers, taking out four B-17s. Blue Flight tackled the bandits as they began a second attack on the rear of the 'Forts', Baker getting behind an Fw 190, which made a steep diving turn in a bid to escape. With four bursts Baker hit the fighter's canopy, fuselage and wing roots. The German aircraft slipped sharply to the left and went into a spin, its pilot probably dead. Baker followed the smoking machine down to 4000 ft, before breaking off to have a go at another Fw 190 coming at him head-on. He fired a short burst at the bandit, then lost sight of it.

Climbing back to 10,000 ft, Baker saw that his wingman was in a scrap with an Fw 190, so he joined in. As the fighter entered a diving turn, it was hit by two bursts from Baker's P-51. Levelling out at 2000 ft, the German bailed out. The abandoned Fw 190 gradually lost altitude, bounced off the ground and carried on flying over a wood. Two Mustangs from the 361st FG made passes on the Fw 190 before it bellied in on a second field, slid into a line of trees and caught fire.

In exchange for its 12.5 victories claimed on the last day of 1944, the 359th suffered one loss. Lt Donald L Murphy (in P-51D-5 44-13786) of the 368th was killed in an unexplained crash near Grossenheim.

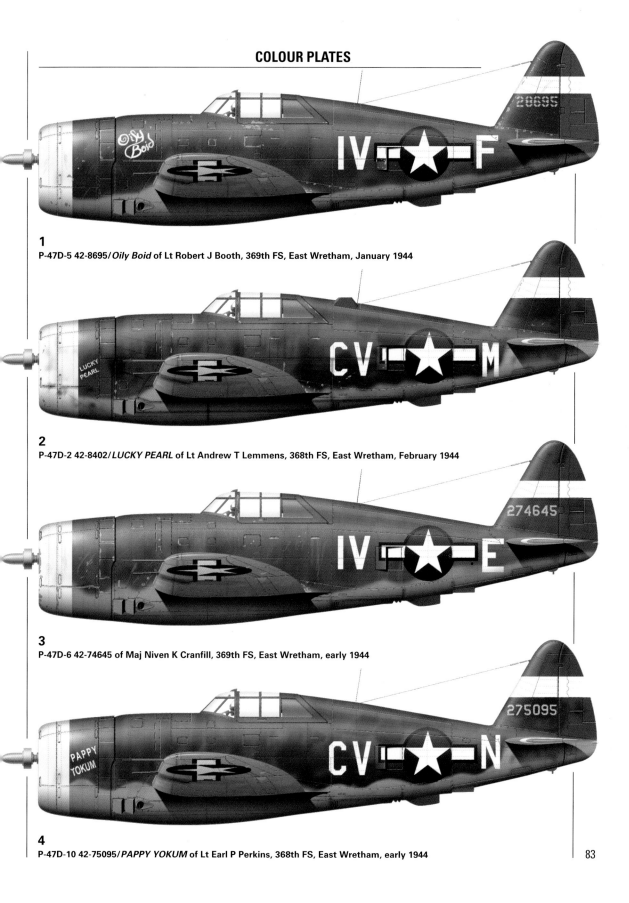

1
P-47D-5 42-8695/*Oily Boid* of Lt Robert J Booth, 369th FS, East Wretham, January 1944

2
P-47D-2 42-8402/*LUCKY PEARL* of Lt Andrew T Lemmens, 368th FS, East Wretham, February 1944

3
P-47D-6 42-74645 of Maj Niven K Cranfill, 369th FS, East Wretham, early 1944

4
P-47D-10 42-75095/*PAPPY YOKUM* of Lt Earl P Perkins, 368th FS, East Wretham, early 1944

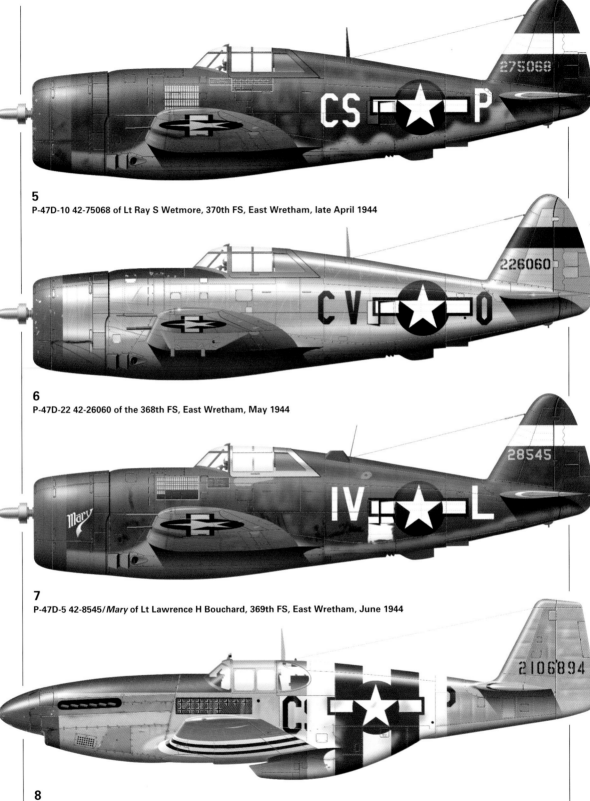

5
P-47D-10 42-75068 of Lt Ray S Wetmore, 370th FS, East Wretham, late April 1944

6
P-47D-22 42-26060 of the 368th FS, East Wretham, May 1944

7
P-47D-5 42-8545/*Mary* of Lt Lawrence H Bouchard, 369th FS, East Wretham, June 1944

8
P-51B-15 42-106894 of Lt Ray S Wetmore, 370th FS, East Wretham, June 1944

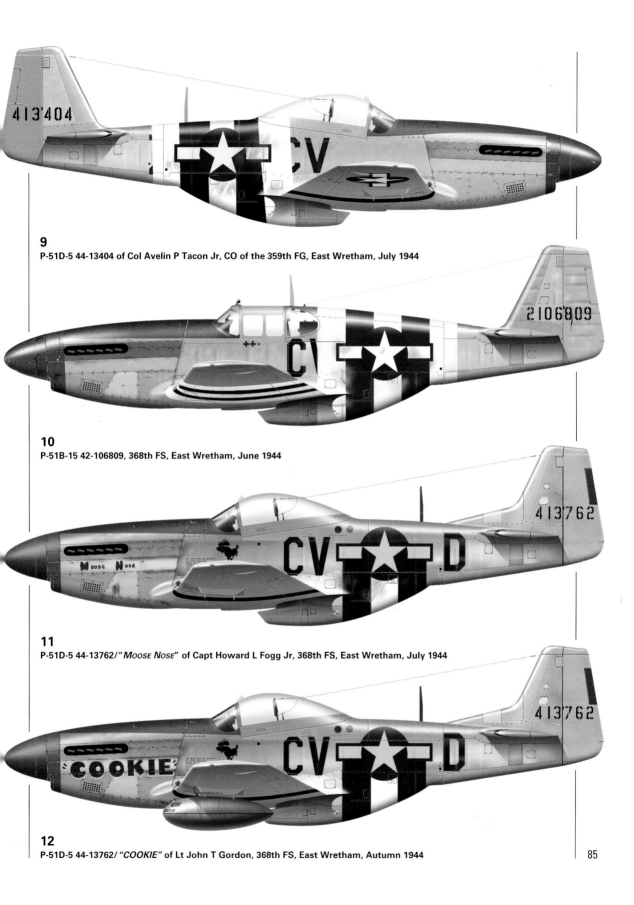

9
P-51D-5 44-13404 of Col Avelin P Tacon Jr, CO of the 359th FG, East Wretham, July 1944

10
P-51B-15 42-106809, 368th FS, East Wretham, June 1944

11
P-51D-5 44-13762/"*Moose Nose*" of Capt Howard L Fogg Jr, 368th FS, East Wretham, July 1944

12
P-51D-5 44-13762/ *"COOKIE"* of Lt John T Gordon, 368th FS, East Wretham, Autumn 1944

13
P-51D-5 44-13669/*Pegelin* of Lt Glenn C Bach, 368th FS, East Wretham, July 1944

14
P-51B-10 42-106581/*TOOTSER* of Lt John S Keesey, 368th FS, East Wretham, August 1944

15
P-51D-5 44-13390/*DEVILESS 3* of Maj Nevin K Cranfill, 369th FS, East Wretham, August 1944

16
P-51D-5 44-13606/*LOUISIANA HEAT WAVE* of Lt Claude J Crenshaw, 369th FS, East Wretham, September 1944

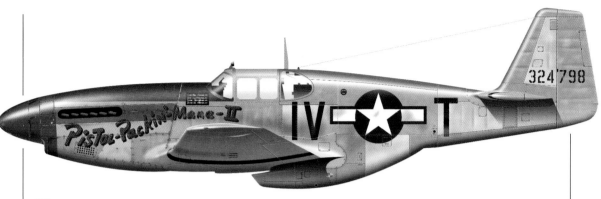

17
P-51B-15 43-24798/*PisToL-Packin'-Mama-II* of Lt Harry L Matthew, 369th FS, East Wretham, October 1944

18
P-51D-10 44-14521 of Lt Col Daniel D McKee, CO of the 370th FS, East Wretham, November 1944

19
P-51D-15 44-14965/*NANCY* of Col John P Randolph, CO of the 359th FG, East Wretham, November 1944

20
P-51D-15 44-14965/*LADY* of Col John P Randolph, CO of the 359th FG, East Wretham, early April 1945

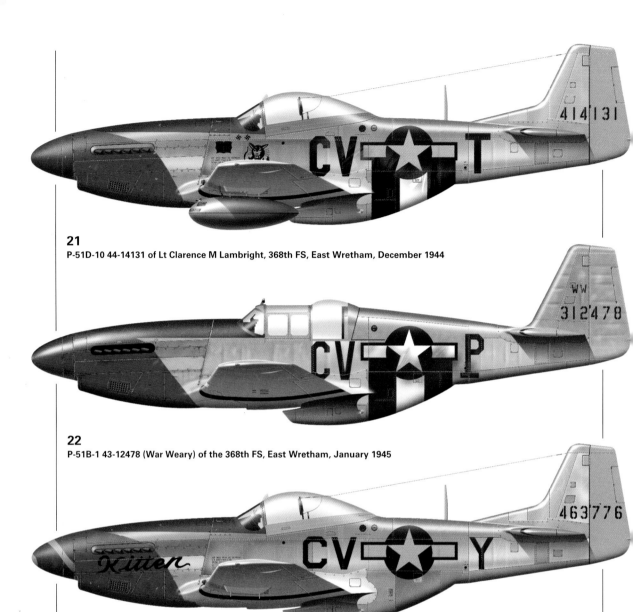

21
P-51D-10 44-14131 of Lt Clarence M Lambright, 368th FS, East Wretham, December 1944

22
P-51B-1 43-12478 (War Weary) of the 368th FS, East Wretham, January 1945

23
P-51D-20 44-63776/ *Kitten* of Lt George W Long Jr, 368th FS, East Wretham, January 1945

24
P-51D-20 44-63689/ *"POP" my boy* (right side), *FRITZIE VI* (left side) of Lt John T Marron, 368th FS, East Wretham, January 1945

25
P-51D-15 44-15717/ *WILD WILL* of Lt Col James W Parsons, 368th FS, East Wretham, February 1945

26
P-51D-15 44-15102/ *JOSEPHINE II* of Capt Jimmy C Shoffit, 370th FS, East Wretham, 1945

27
P-51D-10 44-14625/ *Pauline* of Lt Lee Patton, 369th FS, East Wretham, February 1945

28
P-51D-15 44-15711 of Capt John F Collins Jr, 368th FS, East Wretham, February 1945

29
P-51D-10 44-14733/*Daddy's Girl* of Capt Ray S Wetmore, 370th FS, East Wretham, March 1945

30
P-51D-5 44-11222/*Evelyn* of Lt Frank Rea Jr, 368th FS, East Wretham, March 1945

31
P-51K-5 44-11685/*Janet* (left side), *Elva May* (right side) of Lt John D Cooley Jr, 368th FS,
East Wretham, 1945

32
P-51D-10 44-14127/*DilBert* (left side), *Lil' Marge* (right side) of Lt Robert W McIntosh, 369th FS, East Wretham, March 1945

33
P-51D-15 44-15015/ *"Babe"* of Lt Vernon T Judkins, 369th FS, East Wretham, 1945

34
P-51K-5 44-11574/*MARILYN BETH* (left side), *Miss Virginia* (right side) of Capt William F Stepp,
370th FS, East Wretham, 1945

35
P-51D-20 44-72425/*Gloria Mac* of Lt Robert E McCormack, 369th FS, East Wretham, March 1945

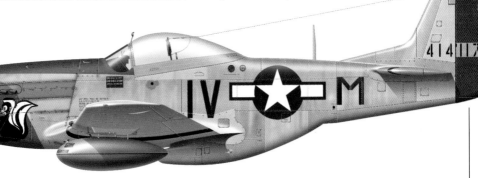

36
P-51D-10 44-14117/*Stinky* of Lt Joseph W Mejaski, 369th FS, East Wretham, March 1945

37
P-51D-15 44-15371/ *"HAPPY"* of Capt James L Way Jr, 368th FS, East Wretham, March 1945

38
P-51D-15 44-15215/ *TORCHY* of Flt Off Harley E Berndt, 369th FS, East Wretham, March 1945

39
P-51D-20 44-72067/ *OLE' GOAT* of Maj George A Doersch, 368th FS, East Wretham, April 1945

40
P-51D-25 44-72746 of Lt Col Donald A Baccus, CO of the 359th FG, East Wretham, April 1945

41
P-51D-15 44-14870/*PETER E. Jr.* of the 368th FS, East Wretham, April 1945

42
P-51D-20 44-72208/*DELECTABLE* of Lt Emidio L 'Dago' Bellante, 370th FS, East Wretham, April 1945

43
P-51D-5 44-13893/*Caroline* of Capt Thomas P Smith, 370th FS, East Wretham, April 1945

44
P-51D-20 44-72366/*HUBERT* of Lt Rene L Burtner, 369th FS, East Wretham, May 1945

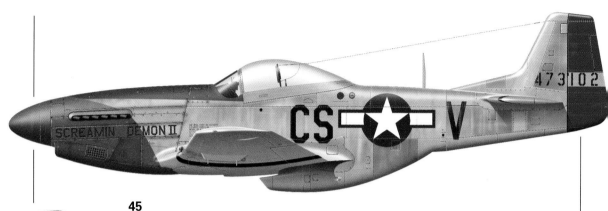

45
P-51D-25 44-73102/*SCREAMIN DEMON II* of Capt Andrew T Lemmens, 370th FS, East Wretham, 1945

46
P-51D-15 44-15277/ *"CisCo"* of the 370th FS, East Wretham, early Autumn 1945

47
P-47D-6 42-74676/*Blondie II* of the 370th FS, East Wretham, Summer 1945

48
P-47D-2 42-8381 (War Weary)/*Little One* of the 3rd Gunnery and Tow-Target Flight, East Wretham, early 1945

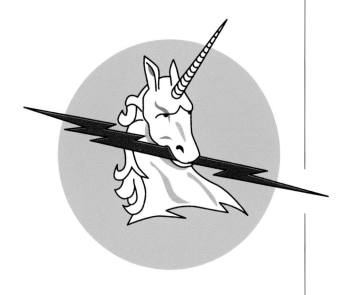

1
359th Fighter Group

2
368th Fighter Squadron

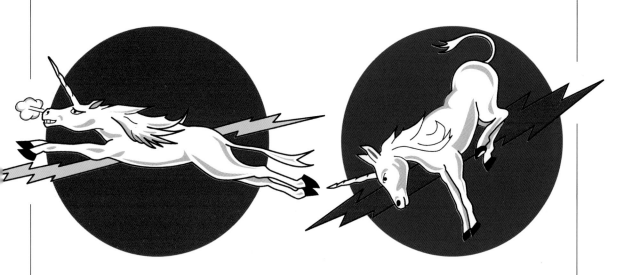

3
369th Fighter Squadron

4
370th Fighter Squadron

1

2

3

4

NEW YEAR

O n 1 January Lt Col Roy Evans led 'A' group and Maj Daniel McKee 'B' group as B-17s hit the oil refineries at Magdeburg once again. The latter formation met up with its charges east of the German town of Meldorf at 1115 hrs, and was attacked within minutes by two Me 262s and six Bf 109s. As a result of this engagement 'B' group lost contact with the bombers. At 1131 hrs, near Lüneburg, about 30 Fw 190s and Bf 109s, as well as four Me 262s, were engaged. The 370th made the only claims during the fight, with Capt Wetmore chasing and destroying a Bf 109 and Capt York 'bagging' an Fw 190. This would be York's last victory, and it made him an ace.

Part of 'A' group rendezvoused near Ratzeburg at 1145 hrs, but broke escort five minutes later when Lt Billy D Kasper of the 368th met a Bf 109 head-on at 32,000 ft while searching for reported bandits. He stalled his Mustang while trying to get into a firing position, then his canopy fogged up. After clearing it, Kasper cut out three other P-51s that were now chasing 'his' Bf 109 and fired from 30 degrees at a distance of just 25 yards. The Messerschmit quickly caught fire and began to disintegrate, then tumbled out of control as the pilot took to his parachute. Kasper and Capt Ralph L Brown were now low on fuel, so along with and Lt John A Denman, whose guns were jammed, they headed for home.

At 1155 hrs, near the German town of Havelberg, Lt Leonard Carter and Flt Off Boyd Adkins Jr of the 368th engaged an Fw 190. Carter

Lt Billy Kasper (right) of the 368th FS poses with his crew chief, S/Sgt Charles Doersom. His aircraft is veteran P-51B-10 42-106619. Kasper completed his 70-mission (325 combat hours) tour in February 1945, having scored one aerial kill – a Bf 109 on 1 January 1945 (*Doersom*)

A Mustang from the 368th FS is waved off from East Wretham in January 1945. Western Europe was then in the midst of the worst winter it had seen in almost a century, and at least five pilots from the 359th FG lost their lives in weather-related crashes in January and February

368th FS armourers (from left to right) Sgt Russell Beamesderfer, Cpls Calvin Fair and Larry Lovell, unidentified crew chief and S/Sgt Neal Cadwalader pose alongside an anonymous P-51D in early 1945. The canvas nose cover draped over the fighter's engine compartment kept moisture from forming in the cylinders, thus making starting easier on cold mornings. The cover also extended back over the canopy, but this one has been pulled forward to show the four kill markings on the canopy frame (*Lovell*)

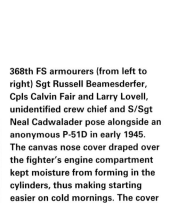

attacked first, scoring hits before his canopy fogged up. Adkins then moved in and secured the kill. At 1200 hrs an Me 262 made a fruitless diving attack on 'A' group near Hamburg.

The 359th was back escorting on the 3rd, this time for B-17s bombing tactical targets around Cologne. Again split into 'A', 'B' and 'C' groups, Lt Col McKee, Lt Col Evans and Maj Hodges were the respective formation leaders. 'C' group's role was a little different to the others, for it was to drop chaff. The bombers failed to show up at the rendezvous point, and after a brief search the 359th pressed on to the target alone, providing area support. Lts William Collins and Arthur Morris of the 369th foiled several attempts by Me 262s to attack the bombers, and then bounced four Fw 190s. During the ensuing chase 'down to the deck', they each destroyed a fighter and shared in the destruction of the remaining two.

On the 14th Lt Col Evans led the 359th on a support mission for B-24s attacking oil facilities at Hemmingstedt. At 1230 hrs they met the bomber crews near Heligoland Island at 31,000 ft, and the subsequent operation

was deemed to be a success – the target was left smoking badly and no bombers were lost. There was no sign of the enemy either. The bombers went on their way at 1300 hrs, freeing up the 359th to seek out ground targets. At 1355 hrs Capt Ettlesen of the 368th strafed a train near Hannover, wiping out the locomotive and damaging ten flat wagons loaded with about 20 staff cars and trucks.

Between 1330 and 1415 hrs, Red and Blue Flights of the 370th took on a group of Fw 190s near Dummer Lake. Capt Wetmore was leading Red Flight when he spotted a bandit doing 'lazy-eights' and chandelles east of Hannover. Red Flight dropped their tanks and chased the German all the way to Dummer Lake, where they broke off the engagement. The flight then headed to an airfield north-west of the lake, but nothing was found.

As they turned back towards Dummer Lake, a call on the radio told them that bandits had been detected in the vicinity of Vorden. Wetmore then spotted four Fw 190s flashing past below him in trail, heading for an airfield, and he immediately bounced them. His first victim was hit from 300 yards out, the pilot dying trying to crash-land his fighter. The ace then struck his second target with a short burst from dead astern at close range. The pilot tried to break, but snapped into the ground and exploded. Victim number three was again taken from the rear, at 300 yards, the Fw 190 spinning into the ground and exploding.

Wetmore then helped his wingman, Lt Rueschenberg, to shoot down another Focke-Wulf by catching it in a cross-fire. The German pilot managed to belly-land his stricken fighter on the airfield, but Wetmore duly strafed it, killing the pilot and setting the wreckage on fire. He then spotted two more Fw 190s being chased by a P-51 from the 339th FG, which nailed one of the bandits – the pilot managed to jump clear. Firing from 400 yards, and with 30 degrees deflection, Wetmore scored hits on the remaining Fw 190 and the pilot bailing out.

Blue Flight of the 370th, led by Capt George 'Pop' Doersch, had arrived on the scene just as Wetmore had scored his third kill. Doersch saw an Fw 190 circling 200 ft above the perimeter of the airfield within the range of 20 mm flak guns, and he and his wingman, Lt Jack McCoskey, ignored the anti-aircraft threat and went after the Fw 190. Doersch quickly downed the enemy fighter, then took on another Fw 190 being chased by four P-51s. The bandit turned into his attack twice, while making for the north side of the airfield, and its protective flak. Doersch made a final pass at the fighter, overshot it and pulled up into the vertical and rolled inverted to see what had happened to his quarry.

Just then McCoskey also overshot the Fw 190, made a tight turn (in P-51D-15 44-15543), went into a high-speed stall (possibly caused by too much fuel in the fuselage tank)

Lt Jack McCoskey (left) became a PoW on 14 January 1945 after his fighter suffered a high-speed stall and hit the ground almost inverted at 400 mph near Vorden airfield. Thrown clear when the Mustang exploded, his only injury was a badly broken jaw. Here, McCoskey discusses a previous engagement with ace 'Pop' Doersch, who also played a prominent role during the 14 January mission. McCoskey had claimed one kill in the air and a shared strafing victory on the ground prior to his capture and snapped into the ground, almost inverted, at 400 mph. His P-51 exploded, but McCoskey was miraculously thrown clear. Taken prisoner, he was hospitalised with a badly broken jaw.

Doersch, meanwhile, hit the Fw 190, and the pilot jettisoned his canopy and bailed out at the top of a hammer-head stall. Believing his friend had been killed, a furious Doersch tried to collapse the German's parachute, but he eventually cooled off and let him land safely.

The group flew escort for B-17s bombing railway targets at Siegen, in Germany, on 29 January, Lt Col Evans leading 'A' group and Maj James Lovett 'B' group. Rendezvousing over Hoorn, in the Netherlands, at 1055 hrs, the bombers delivered their deadly load by radar, with the results being hidden by cloud. The 369th broke escort north of Giessen at 1200 hrs and went off to strafe. During the remainder of the mission pilots damaged 20 wagons and 15 oil tank trucks, six Fw 190 wings on a flat truck, and destroyed a truck and a powerhouse. The 368th finished escort duty at 1215 hrs, and it too went down around Giessen to strafe – their claims included three destroyed locomotives, 20 wagons damaged and the destruction of an oil tanker, three trucks, two staff cars and a powerhouse.

On the debit side, the 368th also suffered the only losses of the mission when Lt Richard Daniels mistakenly strafed an American installation at Ingwiller, in France. During his second pass he was given a warning burst of fire, but he pressed on with the attack and was downed on his third pass. Daniels was killed when his P-51 crashed three miles away at Bauxwiller.

The 368th also lost Lt John M Marr, who was flying his first mission for two weeks on the 29th His P-51 was hit by flak over Germany, and when he bailed out over Sanites, in France, his leg struck the tail of his fighter. Coming down in the centre of town, Marr's parachute snagged on a telegraph pole, leaving him dangling outside a second floor window. Several residents pulled him in, and he was hospitalised locally under the care of one Madam la Comtesse de Dampierre. Marr returned to the 359th a month later.

Although January had seen the group lose just one pilot to enemy action, five others had been killed in operational accidents whilst taking off or returning to East Wretham.

By the beginning of February only eight of the original 86 pilots that had arrived in the ETO with the 359th in October 1943 were still flying – Niven Cranfill, 'Pop' Doersch, Al Homeyer, John Hunter, Dan McKee, Andy Lemmens, Bob Thompson and Ray Wetmore.

In a strange month for the group, the 359th failed to score a single aerial victory. This was partly due to the fact that the Germans were concentrating much of their remaining air power in the east in an attempt to stem the ruthless Soviet advance. Ground attack action, on the other hand, was ferocious, and 14 pilots failed to return from February's 17 missions. Such losses were common among all fighter groups at this late stage of the war, and they became so bad that at the end of the month 67th FW Command ordered a halt to all opportunity strafing.

On 9 February an escort was put up for B-17s bombing synthetic oil facilities at Lutzkendorf, in Germany. The bomber formations were ragged, the target was bombed visually and one 'Fort' was downed by flak. There was no sign of the Luftwaffe in the air, and as the bombers left the target area, Blue Flight of the 368th, led by Capt Ettlesen, did some

Mobile Landing Control is seen in action at East Wretham during the winter of 1944-45. The observation bubble atop the chequered vehicle appears to be a Plexiglas nose fairing souvenired from a nearby B-17 base

strafing. One of two unidentified aircraft parked at an airfield near Gotha was damaged by Ettlesen in the first attack of the mission. Moving on, he quickly destroyed two locomotives, and was banking sharply for an attack on a third when his flight entered a rain squall. As Lt Marvin F 'Frenchy' Boussu emerged from the rain, he spotted a train and made a pass, blowing up the locomotive's boiler.

Someone then realised that the veteran Ettlesen (in P-51K-5 44-11651) was missing, and when attempts were made to contact him by radio and there was no response, the rest of Blue Flight headed home. He was last seen alive making a head-on attack on a train – a poetic epitaph for a pilot who helped write the book on attacking ground targets. Blue Flight of the 370th also strafed, and their claims included eight locomotives destroyed.

Soon after Germany surrendered, Capt Marvin Boussu returned to the US and met Charles Ettlesen's father. On a map, he pointed out the spot where the pilot must have been shot down, and Mr Ettlesen and his new wife immediately travelled to Germany and recovered his son's remains.

On 11 February the group conducted a sweep around the German town of Paderborn. Claims for the day included 24 locomotives destroyed and ten damaged, as well as damage to 111 pieces of rolling stock.

Three days later Lt Cols Evans and McKee led 'A' and 'B' groups as the 359th flew support for B-17s bombing the marshalling yards at Dresden. The pilots again met with no aerial opposition, and after breaking escort they dropped down to strafe. They destroyed 26 locomotives and damaged 12 others, along with 112 wagons, 17 oil tankers, 14 medium tanks on flat trucks, 11 switch houses, six railway buildings and 19 barges.

'A' group paid a high price for this success, however, for Lt Col Evans' Mustang (P-51D-15 44-14894, misnamed *Lucky*!) was hit by flak and lost engine oil pressure. The Merlin duly overheated, forcing the pilot to bail out near Plauen, where he was taken prisoner. Lt Roy W Garrett of the 368th was also captured when his Mustang (P-51D-10 44-14650) developed engine trouble near the Dutch town of Meppel and he bailed out right into the hands of German soldiers.

Prior to this mission being flown, pilots had been issued with small silk Russian flags and identification cards that were to be used in case they had to put down in Russian-held territory.

The marshalling yards at Nürnberg were the escort destination for 'A' and 'B' groups on the 21st, the target being hit through heavy cloud cover and the bombing results remaining unknown. No 'Forts' were lost, even though the flak was heavy. On a pre-arranged signal, the 369th dropped escort and split into two sections to strafe airfields – the 368th and 370th continued to provide escort until just east of Selestadt, at 1245 hrs.

Meanwhile, Red and Yellow Flights of the 369th strafed an airfield near Nordlingen, where Maj Hodges damaged an Fw 200 transport, Lt Thomson hit an Fw 190 and a twin-engined aircraft, Lt Arthur Morris destroyed a Ju 88 and a fuel lorry, and damaged an Me 410 and Lt Fred S McGehee hit another Fw 200 and an Me 410. In a subsequent attack by White and Blue Flights on an airfield at Schweinfurt, Maj Pezda destroyed a multi-engined aircraft, Lt Robert M Francis damaged an Me 410 and Lt Dale E Kelly shot up a hangar. During Francis's attack, a filler cap came off and his windscreen was covered with oil. Pezda and Kelly were also fortunate to have their claims witnessed, for upon returning to base it was found that their gun cameras had not been loaded with film!

22 February 1945 was the first day of Operation *Clarion*, which saw an all-out assault mounted by Allied air forces on the surviving remnants of the German railway and transport systems. The Eighth Air Force took a gamble and ordered its bombers to fly at 10,000 ft – less than half the usual altitude. Maj Pezda and Capt Wetmore led 'A' and 'B' groups, as the 359th again flew to Germany and back escorting a B-17 mission. The targets bombed were around the town of Perleburg.

Lt Russell E Masters of the 369th lost oil pressure (in P-51D-5 44-13610) and bailed out off the coast near Ijmuiden, in the Netherlands. His parachute opened, but he could not be seen in the water. Listed as missing in action, this was his first mission.

Rendezvous was made north-east of Zwolle, in the Netherlands, and minutes later Lt David P Dunmire of the 368th also realised that his engine was cutting out too. With Lt James W McCormack as escort, he dropped down to 10,000 ft, where the Merlin started running more smoothly. The pair then rejoined the squadron, but a few minutes later dropped out again to strafe a locomotive.

They briefly climbed back into position, before targeting an airfield. Flak struck Dunmire's Mustang (P-51K-5 44-11647) in both wings, tail surfaces and engine, and unable to climb, he asked McCormack to go

Two-tour veteran Maj Edwin Pezda served as 369th FS CO from 1 January to 28 February 1945, when he was shot down by ground fire and captured. 'Fox' to some and 'Swami' to others, Pezda was another of the group's West Point men. He had claimed single aerial and strafing kills prior to becoming a PoW

Capt James L Way Jr of the 368th FS stands arm-in-arm with his unnamed crew chief in front of their P-51D-20 *HAPPY 2* (44-72281). This Mustang was supplied to the newly-reformed Italian Air Force post-war

One of the beautiful ladies that once adorned the walls of Wretham Hall. Capt James L Way was the artist, and his work shows the influence of the Vargas and Petty centrefolds that were so popular at the time

up for a position fix. At 20,000 ft, McCormack lost sight of Dunmire, but gave him a heading for friendly territory over the radio. The route took the latter pilot over Düsseldorf, where at 500 ft he was again hit by flak and began losing coolant. Radio contact was lost, and Dunmire was listed as missing in action – this was subsequently altered to killed in action.

North of Gardelegen, near the target area, six Me 262s attacked the 'Forts', downing one before quickly outdistancing the escorting P-51s. This was the only B-17 shot down that day, proving that the fear of high losses at lower altitudes was unfounded.

At 1230 hrs, the 370th bounced a single Me 262 flying low near Pritzwalk. Capt Wetmore and Capt McInnes fired at long range but the German vanished in the haze. One minute later Lt Windmiller spotted an airfield, where he damaged an Me 410 and a decoy aircraft. He and his wingman also noticed a crashed Me 262 on the airfield, and while they were confident it was the one fired on by Wetmore and McInnes, it could not be claimed.

In an overlapping action the 369th's Red Flight strafed an airfield near Parchim, Lt McGehee destroying a Ju 88 and damaging two others, and Lt Harold Tenenbaum damaging one twin-engined aircraft and two horse-drawn wagons. Capt William Collins, meanwhile, destroyed two Ju 88s and damaged another. Finally, a flight from the 369th shared in the destruction of two locomotives and 12 wagons loaded with explosives.

The following day was a black one in the combat history of the 359th FG, for it saw four pilots killed in action whilst providing penetration and withdrawal support for B-17s bombing transportation and rail targets in Zwickau. The 369th's Lt Lawrence Meyer hit a hill (in P-51D-15 44-15394) while strafing a train near Fulda. Lost in the vicinity of the target

The 370th FS scoreboard dominates the squadron's Operations hut. This unit would finish the war as the high-scorers of the 359th FG, being credited with 112 aerial victories. The 369th achieved 82 kills and the 'hard luck' 368th 59.5. The figure to the left is yet another of James Way's 'painted ladies'

A big-time strafer on 24 October 1944 was Lt Harry Matthew from West Virginia, who is seen in the photograph above exiting his P-51B-15 *PisToL-Packin'-Mama-II* (43-24798) – this aircraft went to the 361st FG after 'Matt' switched to P-51D-15 44-15081, named *PisToL-Packin'-Mama-III*. He shared in the destruction of ten locomotives with various teams in the 369th FS. Matthew was well into his second tour when he flew 44-15081 through power lines while attacking a train on 28 February 1945. He bailed out and was taken prisoner, but was liberated three weeks later

were the 370th's Capt Washington Lyon (in P-51D-15 44-14987) and Lt Malcolm Paulette (in P-51D-10 44-14773), both of whom simply dropped out of formation near the target area. The final loss was also suffered by the 370th, when recently-arrived Lt Garland McGregor flew into overcast near East Wretham whilst flying radio relay. His fighter hit the ground at nearby Watton.

The mission on 28 February was a fighter sweep around Munich. Group CO Col John Randolph was in charge, and of the 44 Mustangs that took off only one came home early. The 359th arrived over the target area at 0930 hrs and at 14,000 ft. For the 368th, Lt George W Long destroyed a locomotive and damaged four others, as well as five wagons, near Ingolstadt. Lts John Collins Jr and John D Cooley Jr teamed up to damage another locomotive and two wagons, and they also made two passes on a wood yard, starting two fires. Between Augsburg and Gunzburg, Lts Allan G Martin and George H Blackburn caught two lorries each towing a Bf 109 on the autobahn. Martin destroyed one of the fighters and its tow lorry, plus another lorry further along the road, while Blackburn destroyed the other Bf 109/vehicle combination.

369th FS CO Maj Ed Pezda was strafing a convoy of lorries near Kunzelsau when ground fire severed an oil line (in P-51D-10 44-14625), forcing him to bail out. He was duly captured. Minutes later Capt Harry Matthew, also from the 369th, flew through some power lines (in P-51D-15 44-15081) while attacking a train near Neustadt and lost his coolant. A two-tour veteran, Matthew was flying his 119th mission (436 combat hours) when he was forced to bail out. Made a PoW, he was freed three weeks later by American ground forces.

The new month of March brought with it shortages of 0.50-cal armour-piercing incendiary ammunition, so practice firing was strictly forbidden. As if that was not bad enough, groundcrews simultaneously experienced a dramatic rise in the number of engine changes required due to the use of 150 octane 'pep-gas'. Formulated to keep spark plugs clean, it created its own problems, however – burned valve seats and stretched valve stems.

It was not all bad news though, for the first P-51D-20 Mustangs arrived at East Wretham on 6 March, and the next day the pilots were briefed on the tail warning radar that was to be installed in their aircraft.

On the 10th the 359th escorted B-17s sent to bomb the marshalling yards at Hagen and Schwerte. Lt Col McKee led 'A' group and Capt Cox 'B' group, their meeting point with the 'Forts' being over the Dutch town of Egmond at 1210 hrs. There was solid cloud cover over the targets, and the bombs had to be dropped by radar. During the mission the 370th searched for jets reported over Koblenz, but found nothing. Escort was maintained until south-east of Koblenz, when a message came through ordering the group to an area east of the Remagen bridgehead. A second call directed the 359th specifically to the Ludendorff bridge at Remagen to search for Fw 190s and Ar 234 jet bombers attacking the span.

Unfortunately the American anti-aircraft gunners at the bridge were not told about the approaching Mustangs, and the 359th came under intense friendly fire, as well as fire from a German 20 mm flak gun situated on a nearby hillside. At 1525 hrs two Mustangs from the 368th, flown by Lts George H Blackburn (in P-51D-15 44-15067) and James W McCormack (flying P-51D-20 44-63740) were both hit by the German

On 10 March 1945, the 368th's Lts James W McCormack (top) and George H Blackburn Jr (bottom), died when their Mustangs were shot down by a German 20 mm flak site positioned on a hillside at Remagen, in Germany. Several historians have mistakenly stated that both men were hit by friendly fire, as an American flak battery was also sited nearby. Prior to their deaths, McCormack had shared in the destruction of six locomotives and Blackburn had been credited with one aircraft destroyed on the ground

Ray Wetmore's most successful fighter was P-51D-10 44-14733, christened *Daddy's Girl*. He scored nine of his 21.25 aerial kills in this machine between 2 November 1944 and 14 January 1945. His first assigned 'bubble-top', the fighter is seen at different stages in its career in these two photos. The top shot reveals kill markings both on the fuselage and canopy rail, as well as a stencilled serial number on the tail and the blue field of the insignia masked off in preparation for the application of a fresh coat of white paint. In the bottom photo the serial number has been touched up to remove the stencilling breaks

guns at 1000 ft. McCormack died when his P-51 crashed soon after being hit, and Blackburn perished when his fighter crashed into a wood near Windhagen, two-and-a-half miles away.

Capt Wetmore's Mustang was also hit, but by the American gunners. A fire started in the right wing of his machine, but this soon died out and the ace flew to St Trond, in Belgium, and bellied in with fuel starvation problems and a jammed canopy. The latter had failed to jettison when it became snagged on a camera installed behind the armour plate aft of the pilot's head. The drill was to crank the canopy back past the point where the cross-brace would catch on the camera *before* jettisoning it. Wetmore evidently failed to follow this procedure! He returned to base on the 12th.

Lt John F 'Bum' McAlevey saw Wetmore in trouble that day, and this was his reaction to the official account of the incident;

'To simply say he was shot up by flak and forced to belly-land his aeroplane misses entirely the drama of being trapped in a burning aircraft.

It omits the fact that he was on fire, and the additional fact – which did nothing for his nerves or self-confidence after he bellied in – that ground personnel at St Trond had to use crowbars to get the canopy off the fighter so that he could get out.'

On 13 March Capt Lemmens of the 370th took long-serving group 'exec' Lt Col Grady L Smith up in the 368th's locally-modified two-seat P-51B to inspect an airfield at Cambrai, in France. However, speculation about a possible move by the group to the Continent came to nothing.

Two day later the 359th escorted B-17s sent to bomb the marshalling yards at Oranienburg, north of Berlin, as well as the Army Headquarters in the capital. Rendezvous was made over Zwolle at 1326 hrs.

At 1500 hrs Capt Wetmore was leading Red Flight of the 370th when he spotted two Me 163s circling at 20,000 ft near Wittenberg. Chasing after one of the rocket fighters, his quarry went into a 70-degree climb at full power. Suddenly, the rocket motor cut out, and the German pilot

The 368th FS's two-seat P-51B-1 43-12478 was photographed at East Wretham on 18 December 1944. Despite being declared War Weary, and relegated to training duties, the fighter remained armed following its unit-level conversion into a two-seater – note the tape over the gunports and the gunsight in the cockpit. Topping off this professional conversion was a sliding Malcolm hood. 43-12478 was used by Capt Andrew Lemmens to fly Lt Col Grady L Smith to Cambrai, in France, on 13 March 1945. They were scouting bases as part of a plan to shift the 359th to France or Belgium, but the move never happened

107

headed for the deck. Wetmore's encounter report details what happened next;

'South-west of Berlin, I saw two Me 163s circling at about 20,000 ft some 20 miles away, in the vicinity of Wittenberg. I flew over towards them, and while at 25,000 ft started after one a little below me. When I got to within 3000 yards he saw me, turned on his jet and went up in a 70-degree climb. At about 26,000 ft his jet quit and he split-essed. I dove with him and levelled off at 2000 ft at his "six o'clock". During the dive my IAS (Indicated Air Speed) was between 550 and 600 mph. I opened fire at 200 yards. Pieces flew off all over. He made a sharp turn to the right and I gave him another short burst. Roughly half his left wing flew off and he caught fire. The pilot bailed out and I saw the craft crash into the ground.'

Wetmore had fired off 222 rounds of API for his last kill, and it was the only enemy aircraft shot down by the entire VIII Fighter Command command that day. Wetmore ended the war as the 359th's top ace. with 21.25 aerial kills and 3.333 strafing victories. He was also the top-scoring active duty ace in the Eighth Air Force come VE-Day.

On 18 March, the 359th again divided into 'A' and 'B' groups to lay on escort for B-17s hitting the marshalling yards at Berlin. The former consisted of 18 P-51s from the 369th, and was led by Capt Ralph Cox, whilst the latter was made up of 34 P-51s from the 368th and 370th, led by Capt Wetmore – six fighters from 'B' group aborted.

'A' group left the 'Forts' at Dummer Lake and made a sweep north-east to Berlin, while 'B' group stayed with the bombers. An Me 262 was spotted 60 miles west of the capital, and a pilot from the 368th gave chase until his P-51 developed a runaway propeller. At 1110 hrs the target was bombed, but a haze reaching up to 30,000 ft hid the results.

Meanwhile, 'A' group ran into flak as it passed over Tempelhof airport at 18,000 ft, causing Yellow Flight to become separated from the rest of the 369th. Capt Cox led Red, White and Blue Flights north to Stettin, and swept down the River Oder to Königsberg. Cruising at 10,000 ft, Cox

Lt Robert J Guggemos of the 369th FS was real a scrapper, which earned him the nickname 'Wolverine'. Guggemos, who arrived in the ETO in October 1944, and later tranferred to the 368th FS, finished his tour in September 1945 with an Me 262 kill in the air and two strafing victories

Flt Off Harley E Berndt damaged a Yak-9 on 18 March in a one-sided clash between the 359th FG and the Soviet Air Force over eastern Germany. Berndt, who saw service with the USAF post-war, named all his fighters – ranging from the P-51 through to the F-106 – *TORCHY* (*Berndt*)

The 369th's Lt Robert W McIntosh and his groundcrew pose with their P-51D-10 *DilBert* (44-14127). Crew chief S/Sgt Floyd Myers is standing on the left, McIntosh in the centre and assistant crew chief Sgt Robert Pollak on the right. McIntosh was flying P-51D-20 *Gloria Mac* (44-72425) when he downed his Yak-9

spotted two unidentified aircraft heading south-east, and he led the P-51s in pursuit. The bogies were caught over an airfield at Zackerick, north of Kustrin, and they were quickly identified as Russian Yak-9s.

Moments later four other fighters were spotted over the same airfield, and these had radial engines. It was assumed that they were Fw 190s attacking the field. The 369th made a diving attack, Lt Robert J Guggemos latching on to what he identified as an Fw 190 and firing on it from 500 yards, without scoring any hits. As he moved in closer, both fighters entered a haze, and when it cleared he found himself behind a Yak-9. Guggemos tried to break off the tussle, but the Yak pilot became aggressive, got on his tail and started firing. Guggemos's wingman, Lt Robert McCormack, clobbered the Yak in the wing roots and it disintegrated. The Americans climbed to 12,000 ft and watched as the sky below them filled with burning fighters.

In the meantime, Cox was leading an attack on the four fighters thought to be Fw 190s. Cox singled out the leader of the flight and fired a long burst from 90 down to 40 degrees deflection, scoring heavily and causing the fighter to burst into flames and crash. He then quickly destroyed two more fighters before being told that he was fighting the Russians. The leader of Red Flight, Lt Rene Burtner, also scored a kill at this time. Cox was later officially credited with a solitary Fw 190 victory, which gave him five aerial kills exactly.

Lt Robert Gaines Jr was leading Yellow flight to the same general area when they bounced what appeared to be three Bf 109s near Joachimsthal. As they closed in on the trio, which was flying at 2000 ft, the bogies went into a diving left turn. Gaines fired a long burst into the lead aircraft, which was bluish in colour, and with no visible markings. The stricken fighter plummeted straight into Werbellin Lake and exploded. Flt Off Harley E Berndt (Yellow 4) damaged the number two in the flight, scoring hits in the wing roots and cockpit, beginning at a range of 600 yards and closing to 200 yards. The bogie then broke right and down and Berndt rejoined his flight.

Lt Bryce H Thomson (Yellow 3) also bounced what he thought was a Bf 109, but as he closed in for the kill he realised it was not a German

aircraft at all. Thomson then noticed that he in turn was being fired on. Breaking hard, he got on the tail of his attacker in one 360-degree turn and identified it as a Yak-9. He then pulled up beside the Yak, waggled his Mustang's wings, pointed to the star insignia and then waved at the Russian pilot. The Russian hesitated, then waved back. Thomson retired and joined another flight of P-51s.

As this was going on, the combat over the airfield continued as Burtner led Red Flight on a strafing pass, during which he torched two Yak-9s taxying out to take off. Lt Robert W McIntosh also fired on a fighter that was landing, and his gun camera film showed a pattern of rounds cutting up the ground between the fighter that was landing and the one taxying. One of these machines then ground-looped.

Capt Wetmore, who had been monitoring the fight on his radio, headed for the scene with 'B' group. He bounced ten bogies flying on the deck, but noticed red stars on their fuselages. Breaking off violently, he narrowly avoided shooting down an La-5. As the fight continued over Zackerick, Maj Cranfill of the 368th bagged two more Yak-9s. By now the Russians were putting up considerable flak, and Cox ordered his pilots to break off combat. The 359th retired without loss, returning home safely.

Soviet leader Marshal Joseph Stalin had the Russian pilots involved in the incident shot, and demanded that his counterpart, President Franklin D Roosevelt, order the execution of all Americans that took part. The only pilot court-martialled was Lt Robert McIntosh, whose gun camera film was the sole evidence of the incident, the other films having been 'lost in the developing tank'.

The story goes that McIntosh was fined a dollar, given a carton of cigarettes and transferred home – he was considered lucky by some of the other pilots, for they remained in England for months after the war, completing their tours and worrying about their fates. They need not have worried, for Lt Gen James H Doolittle, Commander of the Eighth Air Force, was not about to hang any of 'his boys', and eventually the incident died a quiet death.

But how did it happen? The most serious error committed by the 359th pilots was poor aircraft recognition. That said, from the rear, the Fw 190 and La-5 looked similar, as did the Bf 109 and Yak-9, and the little differences between these types were irrelevant when a Russian fighter

Capt Rene Burtner's P-51D-20 *HUBERT* (44-72366) was used by Lt Fred McGehee to shoot down two Bf 109s on 24 March 1945. The stripes on the dorsal strake denote that Burtner was a flight leader. This aircraft was sold to the Swedish Air Force post-war (*Burtner*)

19 March 1945 was Maj Niven Cranfill's day, for not only did he score the 359's only kill, he also 'made ace' to boot. The 'icing on the cake' was provided by the type of aircraft he shot down – a highly prized Me 262. 'Cranny' also damaged a second Me 262 that was attacking a Mustang, thus saving its pilot

Maj Cranfill is seen at the controls of P-51D-15 44-15717, which he used to down his Me 262 on 19 March 1945. This photograph was taken prior to 'Cranny's' 'ace making' engagement, for the Mustang only features four victory symbols on its canopy rail (*Palicka*)

On 22 March 1945 Lt Jack 'Hot Shot Charlie' Schulte of the 370th FS experienced a serious landing accident in his flak-damaged P-51 at East Wretham. The fighter suddenly flipped over during its roll out down the runway, and it took crash crews nearly 30 minutes to extricate Schulte. Fortunately, he emerged without any serious injuries. Note how the paint on the propeller blades has been worn off in the incident, and that the lack of dirt on the tyres indicates that the brakes locked up – possibly the cause of the accident

pilot was determined to kill you. Identification problems were compounded by the fact that the Russians often did not paint the red star insignia on top of their fighters' wings. Furthermore, the Russians were paranoid about telling the Allies just how far they had advanced into Germany, so it is possible that the airfield was still shown as German-held on US maps. One thing is certain – the much-vaunted Yak-9 was definitely no match for the P-51.

The following day the 359th flew area support for B-17s scheduled to bomb Halle. 'A' group was led by Capt Wetmore, while 'B' group was under the leadership of Maj Hodges. Escort and charges met up at 15,000 ft over Sangerhausen at 1307 hrs, and due to poor visibility, the 'Forts' hit secondary targets at Jena (motor transport) and Zwickau (optical works), as well as targets of opportunity.

Maj Cranfill was leading the 368th south of Dessau when, at 1400 hrs, three Me 262s were seen passing overhead. As most of the squadron dropped their tanks to chase them, Cranfill spotted 15 more Me 262s below him, heading south towards a box of 'Forts', which they attacked.

As the jets broke off their attack, Cranfill found himself in the position to bounce them. Seeing one of the Me 262s on the tail of a P-51, he went after it first, scoring hits on the wings, and saving the Mustang. Following the damaged jet north, Cranfill came across another Me 262 and started shooting at it from below and astern, at 600-800 yards. Hit on the bottom of the fuselage, the jet began a diving turn to the left. A second, longer burst struck the spiralling fighter, which hit the ground and exploded. Cranfill had just claimed his fifth, and last, aerial victory

As he watched the jet crash, he also noticed a second explosion on the ground about a quarter of a mile away near Halle. Minutes later he realised that he had just witnessed the death of his wingman, Lt Clifton

111

Maj James W Parsons (wearing a British helmet and 'Mae West') and his crew chief, S/Sgt Floyd Myers. On 24 March 1945 Parsons scored an aerial victory while flying *Wild Will*, which he named in honour of his first squadron commander, Maj William Miller, of the 42nd FS/54th FG, based in the Aleutians. Parsons, who would become the last wartime CO of the 368th FS, having previously served with both the 369th FS and the 359th FG HQ Flight, scored one kill in the air and two on the ground

Capt Robert C Thomson of the 369th FS shot down two Bf 109s on 24 March 1945. A two-tour veteran who completed 123 missions and amassed a massive 540 combat hours, he had scored four kills in the air by VE-Day

Enoch Jr, (flying P-51D-15 44-15371). He had been a member of the 368th FS for just a matter of weeks.

On 20 March Col John Randolph and his men escorted 20 RAF Lancasters sent to bomb a railway bridge at Nienburg. There was a lot of excitement when the pilots heard that the British would be dropping their 22,000-lb 'Grand Slam' bombs, but disappointment set in when the Lancaster dropped 'common' 2000-lb bombs instead. There were many near misses, and a fire was started at the eastern approach to the bridge. But the span was left standing.

On the 22nd the 359th escorted B-17s heading for a German airfield at Alhorn. The target was bombed visually, and was almost totally wiped out – it was described as 'the best bombing ever witnessed by the 359th'. Upon returning to base, the flak-damaged P-51 flown by the 370th's Lt Jack R Schulte flipped over upon landing. It took half-an-hour to get him out, but Schulte emerged without serious injuries.

The group flew three missions on the 24th, the first of which was an area patrol over Hamm. The pilots performed numerous strafing attacks, and claims included seven locomotives destroyed and four damaged, along with ten wagons, six oil tankers, 13 trucks and five staff cars destroyed. The Mustang of the 368th FS's Lt John T Marron was the only one that sustained any particular damage, flak blowing off the right landing flap. Marron nevertheless flew back to base and landed safely.

Pilots from the first mission had not yet got home when the second operation got under way – an area patrol north-east of Hamm. After patrolling for more than an hour, the 369th spotted 15 Bf 109s setting up a landing pattern over the airfield at Eiklon, and they dived on them.

Capts Robert Thomson and William Collins and Lts Robert Lancaster and Fred McGehee each claimed two kills apiece, while Maj James W Parsons and Lts Dale E Kelly, Harold Tenenbaum and Bryce H Thomson 'bagged' one each. Tenenbaum and Kelly also shared a second kill, while Lt Lee Patton damaged two more fighters. The only damage inflicted on the aircraft of the 369th was done by a 20 mm shell that passed through Capt Thomson's P-51. It narrowly missed oil and coolant lines before exiting through the cockpit, where it also missed the pilot.

The third mission was an uneventful support operation for B-17s bombing the airfield at Twente.

Another synthetic oil plant was the target of the day on 26 March, as Col Randolph led B-17 support to Zeitz. Bombing was carried out through breaks in the clouds, and many bombs fell wide of their target. Flak was intense, and the weather on the mission was described by veteran pilots as 'very hazardous, and constituting a greater risk than was warranted by any results that could be obtained'.

On 3 April the 359th had a chance to see some U-boat yards as they flew escort for B-17s heading to Kiel. At 1630 hrs, near Flensburg, Capt Doersch led Red Flight of the 368th in an attack on five suspected bandits. However, these turned out to be Mustangs of the 361st FG, but behind them were three Me 262s closing in for the kill. Lt Olin G Everhart immediately attacked, hitting the fuselage and both wings of one of the jet fighters, which in turn began to burn and then entered a vertical dive and exploded as it hit the ground. Everhart had fired off just 88 rounds of API for his kill. Unfortunately for him, the victory was not officially awarded.

A jet airfield at Obershleischeim, north of Munich, was the target for the 9th, Lt Col McKee leading off 50 Mustangs, two of which aborted. The fighters met the bombers east of Heidelburg at 1535 hrs, and part of the group maintained a close escort over the target, which was bombed visually with excellent results. At 1600 hrs a flight from the 368th, led by Capt Doersch, timed a strafing run for just after the bombs had hit the targeted airfield. On the first pass Lt Robert H Elliot damaged two Ju 88s, but on his second pass no aircraft were visible due to dust in the air, so he strafed a gun emplacement instead.

At 1645 hrs near Augsburg, on the return leg of the mission, Capt Boussu, who was leading Red Flight of the 368th, spotted three Me 262s starting a head-on attack on some B-17s directly ahead. Red Flight dropped their tanks and moved forward to engage, and the jets switched their attention from the 'Forts' to the Mustangs. The Me 262s zipped past Red Flight, with Red 3 and 4 breaking off in pursuit. Flt Off Raymond C Muzzy and Lt Frank Rea Jr both scored hits, with Muzzy claiming one damaged and one shared damaged with Rea. After the Me 262s

A Bf 109G is lined up in the K-14 sight of the 369th's Lt Dale E Kelly over Eiklon airfield on 24 March 1945. He finished his tour with 1.5 aerial kills to his credit, both of which were scored on this very mission

Lt Harold Tenenbaum of the 369th FS claimed an Me 262 kill during 'The Great Jet Massacre' of 10 April 1945. He had scored 3.5 aerial victories by war's end

These frames were taken from Lt Robert Guggemos's gun camera footage, showing his Me 262 kill on the approach to Gardelegen airfield on 10 April 1945. Seconds later, the ailing jet descended into a steep dive and crashed onto the airfield

outdistanced Muzzy and Rea, Boussu, now at 21,000 ft, spotted them at 10,000 ft. As Red 1 and 2 dived on the three bandits they were seen, and the trailing Me 262 broke right. Boussu fired one burst into its fuselage before it sped off.

At 1650 hrs, while separated from the 368th's White Flight, Lt Leon J Levitt found about 200 Ju 88s parked among the trees beside the autobahn south of Munich. He made two passes, setting two Ju 88s on fire. He also tried to contact his unit by radio but failed, so he left the area.

At 1700 hrs Capt 'Pop' Doersch and his wingman attacked Germering airfield, west of Munich, and on his first pass the ace set an Fw 190 ablaze, and it exploded. On his second pass Doersch pulled out of his attacking dive so low that he could not aim his guns, but he fired them anyway. As he pulled up, his propeller sliced into an He 111 bomber, and at that second a delayed-action bomb exploded beneath him. Flying debris dented the P-51's spinner, cracked the armour-glass windscreen and knocked the rear-view mirror off the windscreen frame. The coolant temperature rose, and he opened both radiator shutters to their maximum aperture, but 50 miles west of Frankfurt the Merlin caught fire and Doersch made a belly landing. Making his way to the American lines, he duly hitched a ride back to base.

On 10 April Capt Cox led 'A' group and Capt Homeyer was in charge of 'B' group as the 359th met up with B-17s over Osnabrück at 1340 hrs and 21,000 ft, before setting off on an escort to hit munitions dumps and Army Headquarters at Oranienburg. Capt Boussu and Lt John T Marron, both from the 368th, briefly chased an Me 262 near Wittstock, with Marron scoring hits on the jet's aft fuselage. The enemy pilot then dived, leading the Mustangs into flak that put paid to the pursuit. In the same area the 370th saw five Me 262s attack the 'Forts', with two of the bandits falling to the bombers' gunners.

Bombing took place at 1450 hrs with good results, although a savage fight for the the skies continued all around the 'heavies'. Lt Tenenbaum of the 369th, and his wingman, Lt Albert S Freeman, were cruising at 14,000 ft when a B-17 exploded right in front of them. Tenenbaum then spotted six Me 262s attacking the 'Forts' above him, so he climbed to engage. Upon reaching 16,000 ft, he spied another Me 262 below him being chased by Mustangs. Abandoning his climb, Tenenbaum also dived after the fleeing fighter, closing the gap until the German started a shallow climb and sped off.

Tenenbaum then noticed two more jets below him, distantly pursued by more Mustangs. Diving from 8000 ft, he closed on one of the bandits and began firing from 500 yards at 60 degrees deflection. As the German pilot lowered his jet's landing gear in preparation to land at Gardelegen airfield, Tenenbaum closed to 100 ft and set the Me 262's right engine on fire. The fighter touched down mid-field, rolled 400 yards and exploded.

The American pilot then caught a second Me 262 trying to land, and fired home some hits before being driven off by flak. As Tenenbaum exited, Lts Guggemos and Horace E Garth III from the 369th arrived just in time to engage a third jet that was trying to land. Guggemos pulled in behind it and, closing to 100 ft, fired a long burst. The jet burst into flames, went into a steeper glide and crashed onto the airfield. Lt Ralph R Klaver also damaged an Me 262 at around this time.

Upon learning that flak had driven his wingman Garth off, Guggemos joined Mustangs from the 361st FG heading west, and helped them strafe an airfield at Dannefeld. Eight or nine Bf 109s were left wrecked.

10 April 1945 is known as the day of 'The Great Jet Massacre', with the Eighth Air Force claiming 20 Me 262s destroyed in the air. Total losses for the Luftwaffe on this day were 311 aircraft destroyed and 237 damaged, while the 'Mighty Eighth' lost 19 bombers and eight Mustangs.

Ex-356th FG ace Lt Col Donald A Baccus led the 359th for the first time on 13 April, as the group kept B-17s company on a raid on marshalling yards at Neumünster, followed by strafing. Rendezvous, at 1500 hrs was over the North Sea, and the 370th stayed with the bombers until they dropped their loads 30 minutes later. No enemy aircraft were encountered, and only one bomber was lost.

The 368th went on to strafe targets south of Neumünster, Blue Flight hitting an airfield and three pilots getting four kills each – Lt John

Lt Col Donald Baccus became the 359th FG's final wartime CO on 7 April 1945, and he remained in command until 16 September. He was posted in from the 356th FG, where he had led the 359th FS from June 1943 until April 1944. Baccus then became Deputy CO of the 356th FG, and also led the group for a short time in late 1944. He scored all five of his aerial victories with the 356th FG, 'making ace' on Christmas Day 1944. Baccus also claimed four ground kills, one of which he scored with the 359th FG on 17 April 1945

A Denman 'bagged' four Bf 110s (plus a locomotive later on), Lt Kenneth E Barber got three Bf 110s and an unidentified single-engined aircraft and Lt John W Herb two Bf 110s and two Do 217s destroyed.

The latter pilot struck some trees and tore the ventral scoop off his Mustang (P-51D-20 44-72260) while making a final pass on the airfield. Herb tried to force-land in a nearby field, but fell short by 30 yards and hit more trees. The shattered fighter immediately burst into flames and the young pilot perished in the burning wreckage.

Red Flight from the 368th, led by Capt Doersch, strafed between Lübeck and Neumünster and destroyed four locomotives, while the unit's Yellow Flight struck an air depot at Lüneburg. Capt Hunter bagged an He 111 and Lt Garland E Madison destroyed an Me 410 and an unidentified single-engind aircraft.

Thirteen Mustangs from the 370th strafed around Ratzeburg and Schwerin Lakes, Lt Col McKee and Lt Madison H Newton destroying two Arado Ar 196 floatplanes apiece. Other 370th claims included 11 locomotives destroyed and three damaged.

On the 16th Capt Cox of the 369th led 'A' group on a strafing mission to Prague, in Czechoslovakia. The 368th's Capt Hunter, meanwhile, headed up 'B' group as it provided target support for B-17s bombing the marshalling yards at Platting and Regensburg, followed by strafing.

'A' group found large numbers of aircraft around Prague, where they were protected by heavy flak – no attempt was made to strafe. Meanwhile,

This photo was taken at East Wretham in the final weeks of the war in the ETO. First in the line-up of 368th FS aircraft is P-51D-15 44-15711, which was flown by Lt J F Collins Jr when he took part in strafing missions on 28 February and 3 March 1945. Next in line is P-51D-5 *Sweet Sue* (44-11222), used by Lt Emory Cook to down a Bf 109 on 23 December 1944

A Congressional fact-finding committee visited East Wretham in April 1945. These men are, from left to right, Col John P Randolph, three congressmen from Pennsylvania, Lt Col Donald Baccus and Lt Col Grady Smith. The Mustang is P-51D-15 *PETER E. Jr* (44-14870) of the 368th

Another line of 368th FS Mustangs. Nearest the camera is P-51D-20 *Kitten* (44-63776), in which Lt Douglas A McLean perished when it crashed and burst into flames while attempting a second take-off on 16 January 1945 – this would have been McLean's first mission. Second in line is P-51D-15 *LADY* (44-14965), then P-51K-5 *Silky* (44-11758), flown by Capt John A Denman. Fourth is P-51D-20 *Happy 2* (44-72281) and fifth P-51D-15 *Wild Will* (44-15717) (*Almasy*)

Lt Vernon T Judkins's P-51D-15 *"Babe"* (44-15015), which he flew for almost a year

'B' group witnessed accurate bombing at Platting, before the fighters dropped down to strafe. At 1555 hrs the 368th, less Blue Flight, strafed an airfield next to the target, but the dust from the bombs hitting the nearby marshalling yards had not settled sufficiently enough for the 368th to make anything more than a single pass. Nevertheless, 20 Bf 109s that were inexplicably parked wingtip to wing-tip, presented themselves as an excellent target in the haze, and the American pilots duly destroyed no fewer than five of them and damaged two more.

The 359th split into 'A' and 'B' groups again on the 17th for two missions, the former, led by Lt Col Baccus, flying a series of strafing attacks between Prague, Linz and Salzburg. 'B' group, led by Maj James W Parsons, provided the escort for B-17s raiding the railway yards at Dresden. Rendezvous took place over Coburg at 1330 hrs, and 30 minutes later Capt Collins and his wingman, Lt McGehee, bounced an Me 262 shadowing the bomber stream some 30 miles west of the German city. They gave up the chase after five minutes and returned to the 'Forts'. At 1456 hrs, the two fighter pilots dropped down to investigate a bandit reported near an airfield. Collins found the field, and spotted a well-camouflaged Fw 190 parked there. He destroyed it on his first pass, and decided to get out when he saw tracers coming at him.

At 1345 hrs the 370th, which was part of 'A' group, began hunting around Prague. Three airfields north-east of the city were each found littered with the wreckage of more than 100 enemy aircraft, so Lt Cols Baccus and McKee strafed the fields at Ganacker and Platting, in Germany, instead. At Ganacker, McKee destroyed an Fw 190 and at Platting Baccus wiped out an unidentified twin-engined aircraft and damaged a Bf 109.

Lt John D Cooley Jr poses with crew chief S/Sgt Charles Doersom in front of his P-51K-5 *Janet* (44-11685), which was named after the pilot's girlfriend

The right side of Cooley's Mustang bore the name *Elva May* in honour of S/Sgt Doersom's girlfriend. This aircraft had large code letters painted on the undersides of its wings in the weeks after VE-Day in an attempt to deter bored pilots from 'buzzing' the English countryside (*Doersom*)

25 April 1945 was the last time the 'Mighty Eighth' flew a heavy bomber mission over Europe, and the order to provide escort caught the 359th off guard, as they were not expecting to fly that day. The target was the Pilzen-Skoda armament works at Pilzen, in Czechoslovakia, and bombing was reported to be excellent, with gigantic clouds of smoke rising up to 10,000 ft. No enemy fighters were met, but seven 'Forts' were lost to flak, three spinning down over the target. Fifteen parachutes were counted, and the airmen were fired on by 20 mm flak guns.

As the 359th returned to base, the P-51D flown by Flt Off Jack D Highfield of the 368th suffered a propeller failure. The pilot bellied his Mustang in on a cratered airfield 12 miles south of Dortmund, and succeeded in making it back to England several days later. When the group returned to East Wretham, Lt Clarence R Brown of the 369th nosed his P-51 over but escaped injury.

The following teletype message was received by the 359th FG at 0940 hrs on 7 May 1945. Sent from Eighth Air Force headquarters, it read;

'1. A representative of German High Command signed the unconditional surrender of all German land, sea and air forces in Europe to the Allied Expeditionary Forces and simultaneously to the Soviet High Command at 1041 hrs Central Europe Time, 7 May, under which all forces will cease active operations at 0001 hrs Bravo, 9 May .'

'2. Effective immediately all offensive operations by Allied Expeditionary Force will cease and troops will remain in present positions.'

A few days later word was passed down that training for transfer to the Pacific would soon commence, but this never happened.

PoWs Lt Elmer N Dunlap and Edward J Maslow of the 370th FS returned to East Wretham in May. They reported that German intelligence had photographs of the 370th's pilot status board, as well as the names of all personnel.

On 19 June Lt James J Ferris III of the 368th was killed when his Mustang (P-51B-15 42-106929) crashed during a simulated combat training flight on 19 June. His body was found near the wreckage at Stoke Ferry, in Norfolk, and it is assumed that his parachute had failed to open after he successfully bailed out. The cause of the crash remains unknown.

Late in June a New York newspaper ran the headline, 'Last of the Eighth Air Force returns to the States'. This came as a shock to the 359th, which was still soundly entrenched at East Wretham! On top of that, the risks were not yet over.

Lt Eugene F Dauchert of the 368th FS, who was temporarily serving with the 3rd Gunnery and Tow-Target Flight at East Wretham, was landing an A-35B Vengeance target tug at Martlesham Heath on 7 July when its engine caught fire. Dauchert bellied the aircraft in and rescued his passenger, 56-mission veteran Lt Shelby Jett of the 361st FS/356th FG. Jett died the following day from his injuries, and Dauchert received first and second degree burns around his face and head. He was later awarded the Soldier's Medal for his heroism in getting Jett out of the burning aircraft despite the risk of an imminent explosion.

On 9 July, on a routine training flight, the P-51 flown by Lt George Turinsky lost oil pressure and crashed six miles west of Great Massingham, in Norfolk. Turinsky only suffered minor cuts and bruises about the face, despite the fact that his Mustang was a total wreck.

Tragedy struck for a final time on 23 July, when Flt Off John H Klug Jr of the 368th fatally crashed soon after taking off in P-51D-5 44-13762. His engine had begun to lose power soon after he departed East Wretham, and when he attempted to return to base he realised that his fighter would not make the runway. Hastily picking out an open field to land on, Klug died moments later when the P-51 rolled inverted and crashed.

The 368th FS, often referred to as 'the hard luck squadron', had suffered its 50th, and last, pilot fatality.

August came to East Wretham, and with it the welcome news that Japan had surrendered. Ironically, morale now hit a low point, as all that remained on the minds of most of the pilots was going home. By this time just 18 Mustangs were available for them to fly, and they were being serviced by just one engineering section.

On 4 November 1945 the remaining personnel who had accumulated enough points to ship home boarded the *Queen Mary* and headed for New York. Those pilots still short on hours transferred to the Ninth Air Force and completed their tours as part of the occupying forces – some returned home as late as September 1946. The 359th FG was then transferred to Camp Kilmer, in New Jersey. The wheel had come full circle, and the group was inactivated on 10 November 1945.

POST-WAR ASSIGNMENTS

When the Air National Guard was activated on 30 January 1946, Army Air Force units which had been stood down were selected to fill the slots created. The 368th FS became the 165th FS, stationed at Louisville, Kentucky, and the 369th resurfaced as the 167th FS at Charleston, West Virginia. Sadly, the 370th FS was not revived. The third squadron forming the new group was the 156th FS from Charlotte, North Carolina. These three units were duly placed under the command of the 123rd FG, based at Louisville. The 123rd was an all-new unit, as the wartime fighter groups were not revived.

The Kentucky and West Virginia ANGs played a significant role in the Korean War, flying F-51s, and four decades later both flew C-130Hs in Operation *Desert Storm*. They are still active today.

APPENDICES

APPENDIX 1

359th FG ACES

Name	Unit(s)	Score (aerial)	(ground)
Maj Ray S Wetmore	370th	21.25	2.333
Maj George A Doersch	370th & 368th	10.5	1.5
Lt Robert J Booth	369th	8	0
Capt Claude J Crenshaw	369th	7	3
Capt Benjamin H King	368th	7*	0
Lt Col John B Murphy	370th	6.75	0
Maj Rockford V Gray	369th	6.5**	0
Lt Cyril W Jones Jr	370th	6	5
Maj Roy W Evans	HQ Flt	6***	0
Lt David B Archibald	368th	5	0
Maj Ralph L Cox	370th & 369th	5	0
Lt Col Niven K Cranfill	368th, 369th, 370th & HQ Flt	5	0
Capt William R Hodges	370th	5	0
Lt Paul E Olson	368th	5	0
Capt Robert M York	370th	5	0
Capt William F Collins	369th	4****	0

Notes

*   3 with 339th FS/347th FG

**   2 with 365th FG and 3 with 371st FG

***   5 with 335th FS/4th FG

**** often credited with 5 kills due to misreading of Victory Combat Board Report, which gave him full credit for two shared kills

APPENDIX 2

359th FG GROUP/SQUADRON COMMANDERS

Group Commanders

Col Avelin P Tacon Jr	15/1/43 to 11/11/44
Col John P Randolph	12/11/44 to 7/4/45
Lt Col Donald A Baccus	8/4/45 to 9/45
Lt Col Daniel D McKee	16/9/45 to 10/45
Maj Andrew T Lemmens	29/10/45 to 10/11/45

Squadron Commanders
368th FS

Lt Col Albert R Tyrrell	3/43 to 21/6/44
Maj Clifton Shaw	22/6/44 to 12/8/44
Maj Niven K Cranfill	12/8/44 to 27/8/44
Maj William C Forehand	31/8/44 to 9/44
Capt Charles E Ettlesen	9/44 to 10/44
Maj Benjamin H King	10/44 to 12/44
Capt Charles E Ettlesen	12/44 to 9/2/45
Lt Col Niven K Cranfill	10/2/45 to 22/4/45
Lt Col James W Parsons	23/4/45 to 22/9/45
Capt Marvin F Boussu	22/9/45 to about 24/9/45
Capt Cosgrove	about 24/9/45 to about 26/9/45
Maj Donald J Walter	about 26/9/45 to 11/45

369th FS

Maj Rockford V Gray	3/43 to 12/43
Lt Col William H Swanson	12/43 to 4/44
Maj Chauncey S Irvine	4/44 to 26/7/44
Capt Lester G Taylor	26/7/44 to 3/8/44
Maj Chauncey S Irvine	3/8/44 to 17/10/44
Maj James A Howard	17/10/44 to 8/11/44
Maj Edwin F Pezda	10/11/44 to 11/11/44
Maj Fred S Hodges	11/11/44 to 1/1/45
Maj Edwin F Pezda	1/1/45 to 28/2/45
Maj Fred S Hodges	28/2/45 to 2/3/45
Maj Ralph A Cox	2/3/45 to 9/45
Capt Rene L Burtner	9/45
Capt Joseph A Webster	9/45 to 11/45

370th FS

Lt Allen C Bears	21/1/43 to 15/3/43
Lt Col John B Murphy	16/3/43 to 1/9/44
Capt James K Lovett	1/9/44 to 11/9/44
Lt Col Daniel D McKee	11/9/44 to 21/4/45
Maj Ray S Wetmore	21/4/45 to 11/45

APPENDIX 3

359th FG HEADQUARTERS PILOTS

Lt Col Niven K Cranfill	7/44 to 8/44
Lt Col Roy W Evans	11/44 to 14/2/45
Maj Rockford V Gray	10/43 to 2/44
Maj Fred S Hodges	3/44 to 9/45
Maj Chauncey S Irvine	2/44 to 4/44
Capt Karl H Kirk	7/44 to 9/44 (transferred out)
Maj Andrew T Lemmens	4/45 to 10/45

Lt Col Daniel D McKee	Autumn 1943 to 2/44, then 4/45 to 9/45
Capt Leslie D Minchew	5/45 to 11/45
Lt Col James W Parsons	11/44 to 4/45
Capt Samuel R Smith	4/44 to 8/44 (transferred out)
Lt Col William H Swanson	4/44 to 10/44
Lt Col James V Wilson	2/45 to 11/3/45 (PoW)

APPENDIX 4

SIGNIFICANT MISSIONS

29 January 1944
First aerial kill on mission No 17

10 February 1944
Group receives letter of commendation from Gen Spaatz for action during mission No 26

26 March 1944
First mission for 'Bill's Buzz Boys'

27 March 1944
Lt Frank Fong, only Chinese-American pilot in the ETO, scores a kill during mission No 57

6 May 1944
First all-Mustang outing, mission No 88

19 May 1944
First trip to Berlin, mission No 96

21 May 1944
First 'Chattanooga Choo-Choo' mission, mission No 98

23 May 1944
First use of P-51Bs as dive-bombers, mission No 102

6 June 1944
On D-Day the group flies six missions

25 June 1944
Operation *Zebra*, mission No 148

14 June 1944
Operation *Cadillac*, mission No 164

28 July 1944
Col Tacon makes first official sighting of Me 163 rocket-powered fighter during mission No 176

1 August 1944
Operation *Buick*, mission No 179

4 August 1944
Three pilots land in Sweden, mission No 182

16 August 1944
370th destroys two Me 163s (the first) in aerial combat during mission No 196

27 August 1944
Lt Lawrence Zizka claims the only kill for VIII Fighter Command on mission No 204

10 September 1944
Combat with Swiss aircraft, mission No 214

11 September 1944
Distinguished Unit Citation for mission No 215

24 October 1944
'Jack-in-the-box' barrage balloons encountered on mission No 241. The 368th also manages to score the only two aerial kills credited to the Eighth Air Force fighter groups on this day

5 November 1944
With all 15 fighter groups of the Eighth Air Force in the air, the 359th accounts for one-third of the locomotives destroyed during mission No 248

18 December 1944
Lts Archibald and Olson become aces in a single day on mission No 269

24 December 1944
An 'He 280' jet is sighted during mission No 270

10 March 1945
Remagen bridgehead incident on mission No 314

15 March 1945
Capt Wetmore scores the only kill made by the entire VIII Fighter Command, which also happens to be the third Me 163 destroyed by the 359th FG, on mission No 318

18 March 1945
Intensive aerial combat with Russian aircraft during mission No 320

20 March 1945
Escort for RAF Lancasters on mission No 322

26 March 1945
Worst weather ever encountered, mission No 330

10 April 1945
'The Great Jet Massacre', mission No 341

COLOUR PLATES

1

P-47D-5 42-8695/*Oily Boid* of Lt Robert J Booth, 369th FS, East Wretham, January 1944

'Posty' was a combat pilot with few peers, and he had eight aerial kills to his credit when flak brought him down and he became a PoW on 8 June 1944. He scored two kills in *Oily Boid*, a Bf 109 on 30 January 1944 and a second Messerschmitt fighter on 25 April 1944. Booth's best day was 8 May 1944, when he claimed three kills flying a P-51B. He left the service after the war, only to subsequently re-enlist as a master sergeant. He eventually became a flight engineer on B-50s and then a maintenance officer, before retiring in 1967.

2

P-47D-2 42-8402/*LUCKY PEARL* of Lt Andrew T Lemmens, 368th FS, East Wretham, February 1944

Lemmens was flying this machine when he strafed an airfield at St Dizier on 24 April 1944. Six days later Lt Raymond B Janney used it to damage two Me 410s on the ground at Bricy.

3

P-47D-6 42-74645 of Maj Nevin K Cranfill, 369th FS, East Wretham, early 1944

'Cranny' scored five aerial kills with the 359th FG, and served in all three squadrons and the HQ flight. He flew two tours consisting of 133 missions totalling 506 combat hours. This P-47 was subsequently christened *Deviless* by Cranfill.

4

P-47D-10 42-75095/*PAPPY YOKUM* of Lt Earl P Perkins, 368th FS, East Wretham, early 1944

One of the 368th's original cadre of pilots, Perkins served with the unit from April 1943 until declared tour-expired (with 300 combat hours in his log book) in August 1944. By then he had attained the rank of captain. This particular aircraft was Earl's first assigned mount in the ETO, and it was one of a series of P-47s named for characters in Al Capp's *Li'l Abner* comic strip

5

P-47D-10 42-75068 of Lt Ray S Wetmore, 370th FS, East Wretham, late April 1944

Wetmore scored two Fw 190 kills in this P-47 on 16 March 1944, the fighter being code CR-S at that time. On 11 April he destroyed a Ju 88 on the ground and damaged two others, again while flying this machine. Finally, on 24 April Wetmore 'bagged' a Bf 109 and was given a third of a kill in a twin-engined aircraft whilst strafing the airfield at St Dizier, again in this P-47.

6

P-47D-22 42-26060 of the 368th FS, East Wretham, May 1944

This late-build 'razorback' P-47 was one of the few natural metal Thunderbolts delivered to East Wretham. Arriving in the midst of the 359th FG's transition onto the P-51B/C, none of them saw combat prior to being handed to Ninth Air Force units.

7

P-47D-5 42-8545/*Mary* of Lt Lawrence H Bouchard, 369th FS, East Wretham, June 1944

We will never know the extent of Bouchard's contribution to the group's overall war effort because of his detestation of paperwork! He simply made no claims, unless forced to do so. *Mary* bears 55 mission markers, and that is all we will ever know because most of the combat reports filed by the 369th during its P-47 era omitted the aircraft serial numbers. Bouchard completed his tour in August 1944, having flown 300 combat hours.

8

P-51B-15 42-106894 of Lt Ray S Wetmore, 370th FS, East Wretham, June 1944

Leading ace of the 359th FG by some considerable margin, Ray Wetmore finished the war with 21.25 aerial kills to his credit and 2.333 strafing victories. 'Smack' scored two double kills in this Mustang, on 19 (two Bf 109s) and 29 (two Fw 190s) May. Wetmore flew two tours, completing 142 missions totalling 563 combat hours. Remaining in the Air Force post-war, he died in an F-86A crash at Otis Air Force Base, Massachusetts, on 14 February 1951. Wetmore was serving as CO of 59th Fighter Interceptor Squadron/33rd Fighter Interceptor Group at the time of his death.

9

P-51D-5 44-13404 of Col Avelin P Tacon Jr, CO of the 359th FG, East Wretham, July 1944

One of the first P-51Ds to arrive at East Wretham, this aircraft's freshly-applied invasion stripes were neither parallel or plumb. Serviced by the 368th FS, this machine was used by Tacon to damage a twin-engined aircraft on the ground on 24 July 1944. 44-13404 was lost on 12 September when Lt Louis E Barnett bailed out over Germany after being shot up by German fighters. The pilot died when his parachute failed to deploy properly.

10

P-51B-15 42-106809, 368th FS, East Wretham, June 1944

Lt Thomas J McGeever shot down a Ju 52/3m with this aircraft on 21 May 1944. Lt Billy D Kasper then used it to share in the destruction of three locomotives on 28 August, and finally Lt Arvy F Kysely damaged an Fw 190 and destroyed three locomotives flying it on 11 September. 42-106809 was finally written off on 7 February 1945 when it suffered a failed propeller governor during a gunnery training flight over the North Sea. Pilot Lt Henry L Thompson took to his parachute, and although seen to land safely in the water ten to fifteen miles off the North Yorkshire coast, rescue aircraft and ships failed to find a trace of him

11

P-51D-5 44-13762/"*MOOSE NOSE*" of Capt Howard L Fogg Jr, 368th FS, East Wretham, July 1944

Fogg once wrote that he felt like an old man (he was 28) when flying with the younger and more talented pilots in his unit. He was a leader held in high regard, and although he never scored a kill, he strafed a lot. Fogg completed his 76-mission 271-combat-hour tour in September 1944, and

123

his aircraft was passed to Lt John T Gordon, who renamed it *"COOKIE"* (see profile 12).

12

P-51D-5 44-13762/ *"COOKIE"* of Lt John T Gordon, 368th FS, East Wretham, Autumn 1944

Gordon also strafed a lot in *"COOKIE"*, but the fighter is best remembered for the mission of 9 April 1945, when Flt Off Raymond C Muzzy used it to damage two Me 262s. Gordon completed his tour in July 1945. Having survived for over a year in the ETO, this veteran fighter had the dubious distinction of being involved in the 359th's last fatal crash in the ETO on 23 July 1945. Flt Off John Klug Jr had just departed East Wretham when he felt a loss of power. Turning back towards his Norfolk base, Klug soon realised he would not make it home and chose instead to make a forced landing in a field. However, the fighter suddenly snapped inverted and crashed, killing Klug outright.

13

P-51D-5 44-13669/ *Pegelin* of Lt Glenn C Bach, 368th FS, East Wretham, July 1944

The name *Pegelin* and the clover leaf were applied on both sides of 44-13669's nose. During his tour, Bach destroyed two aircraft on the ground and flew 102 missions, totalling 303 hours. He remained on active duty until joining the Massachusetts ANG in 1947. In November 1951 Bach went to work for Republic Aviation Corporation as the company's Chief Production Test Pilot, and eventually retired from aviation in November 1970. 44-13669 was lost on 5 October 1944 when Lt Clifford Bartlett dropped his tanks and entered a tight downward spiral from 30,000 ft near Tirlemont, in Belgium. The pilot failed to bail out of his fighter before it hit the ground.

14

P-51B-10 42-106581/ *TOOTSER* of Lt John S Keesey, 368th FS, East Wretham, August 1944

On 8 August 1944 Keesey shot down an Fw 190 and damaged three others while flying this P-51. The following day he destroyed another Fw 190 and was awarded a probable, again flying *TOOTSER*. Keesey completed his tour as a captain, having flown 68 missions totalling 270 hours.

15

P-51D-5 44-13390/ *DEVILESS 3* of Maj Nevin K Cranfill, 369th FS, East Wretham, August 1944

Cranfill's armourer, Sgt Anthony Chardella, painted the nose art on *DEVILESS 3*, which was eventually passed on to Lt Thomas G Bur, who changed its name to *Big Noise from WINNETKA*. Bur shared a Bf 109 kill with Lt John E Keur on 18 September 1944 while flying this P-51.

16

P-51D-5 44-13606/ *LOUISIANA HEAT WAVE* of Lt Claude J Crenshaw, 369th FS, East Wretham, September 1944

Crenshaw shot down three Bf 109s while flying this Mustang on 11 and 18 September 1944. His remaining four aerial kills (Fw 190s) were claimed on 21 November 1944 in P-51D-15 44-15016, which was christened simply *HEAT WAVE*. A fifth Fw 190 downed on the latter date was only awarded as a probable, even though it was seen to

crash in a field. Claude left the service after the war, but soon rejoined. He retired as a lieutenant colonel in 1965, and died of lung cancer in 1972.

17

P-51B-15 43-24798/ *PisToL-Packin'-Mama-II* of Lt Harry L Matthew, 369th FS, East Wretham, October 1944

Matthew's only kill was an Fw 190 that he shot down while flying a P-47. However, his strafing score included seven locomotives destroyed and 23 shared destroyed. Matthew was taken prisoner on 28 February 1945 after flying through power lines while attacking yet another train. He had flown 118 missions, totalling 436 hours, up until he was captured. This particular aircraft was passed on to the 361st FG.

18

P-51D-10 44-14521 of Lt Col Daniel D McKee, CO of the 370th FS, East Wretham, November 1944

This is how McKee's aircraft appeared in November 1944, prior to the name *RAYNER Shine* being applied to its nose. One of the 359th's most experienced mission leaders, McKee scored one kill in the air and four on the ground during his tour. He also shared in the destruction of five locomotives.

19

P-51D-15 44-14965/ *NANCY* of Col John P Randolph, CO of the 359th FG, East Wretham, November 1944

Five-kill ace John Randolph was posted to the 359th from the 20th FG in November 1944, and this was the P-51 issued to him. No combat reports have been found for this aircraft.

20

P-51D-15 44-14965/ *LADY* of Col John P Randolph, CO of the 359th FG, East Wretham, early April 1945

A veteran of the Pacific Theatre, as well as a tour with the 20th FG's HQ Flight, Col Randolph had scored one aerial and four strafing victories during the course of his 26 missions with the 20th FG (flown between July and November 1944), and he had these marked on the canopy rail of his assigned Mustang, 44-14965. This aircraft lost its invasion stripes in early 1945, and simultaneously had its name changed to *LADY*. Note also the application of the 368th's (yellow) squadron colour on the fighter's canopy rail.

21

P-51D-10 44-14131 of Lt Clarence M Lambright, 368th FS, East Wretham, December 1944

Lt Merle B Barth shot down an Fw 190 with this Mustang on 24 October, which accounts for one of its victory markings, and assigned pilot Clarence Lambright shared in the destruction of a Bf 109 with Lt Jack O Flack on 11 September 1944. 44-14131 was lost to flak on 18 December 1944, just minutes after Lt Paul E Olson had brought down five Fw 190s.

22

P-51B-1 43-12478 (War Weary) of the 368th FS, East Wretham, January 1945

Assigned to Lt Emory Cook from June 1944 until declared War Weary several months later, this machine was relegated to training duties until converted at unit-level into a two-seater. Topping off this professional conversion was a sliding Malcolm hood. Unusually, despite being little more than a 'hack', the fighter kept its full four-gun armament.

23

P-51D-20 44-63776/*Kitten* of Lt George W Long Jr, 368th FS, East Wretham, January 1945

Long served with the 368th from December 1944 to September 1945, during which time he destroyed one locomotive and shared in the destruction of eight more. He flew this machine for the first few weeks of his tour. *Kitten* was lost when Lt Douglas A MacLean crashed whilst attempting a second take-off run from East Wretham on 16 January 1945 – participating in his very first operational mission, MacLean was killed when the fighter burst into flames.

24

P-51D-20 44-63689/ *"POP" my boy* (right side), *FRITZIE VI* (left side) of Lt John T Marron, 368th FS, East Wretham, January 1945

Marron flew with the 368th from December 1944 through to September 1945, destroying two Bf 109s on the ground and sharing in the destruction of four locomotives – all while flying this P-51.

25

P-51D-15 44-15717/*WILD WILL* of Lt Col James W Parsons, 368th FS, East Wretham, February 1945

Parsons scored one aerial kill and two on the ground, but not in this P-51. Maj Nevin Cranfill *was* flying this aircraft on 11 February 1945 when he shared in the destruction of four locomotives, and also on 19 March 1945 when he shot down an Me 262 and damaged a second. Parsons named this aircraft in honour of his first squadron commander, Maj William Miller, of the 42nd FS/54th FG, based in the Aleutians. The final wartime CO of the 368th FS, Parsons previously served with both the 369th FS and the 359th FG HQ Flight.

26

P-51D-15 44-15102/*JOSEPHINE II* of Capt Jimmy C Shoffit, 370th FS, East Wretham, 1945

Shoffit did not score a kill during his tour but he did damage an Me 163 on 16 August 1944 while flying a B-model Mustang. *JOSEPHINE II* later became *Skeeter's Scooter*, flown by Lt John F McAlevey.

27

P-51D-10 44-14625/*Pauline* of Lt Lee Patton, 369th FS, East Wretham, February 1945

Pauline was lost on 28 February 1945 when 369th FS CO Maj Edwin F Pezda was shot down by flak while strafing a truck convoy. On 24 March 1945 Patton damaged two Bf 109s while flying a P-51K.

28

P-51D-15 44-15711 of Capt John F Collins Jr, 368th FS, East Wretham, February 1945

Collins shared in the damaging of three locomotives, 12 boxcars, a switch house, a lumber yard and a factory while flying this nondescript P-51. He served with the 368th from

October 1944 through to July 1945, when he transferred home, tour-expired.

29

P-51D-10 44-14733/*Daddy's Girl* of Capt Ray S Wetmore, 370th FS, East Wretham, March 1945

Ray Wetmore's most successful fighter, he scored nine of his 21.25 aerial kills in this machine between 2 November 1944 and 14 January 1945. His first assigned 'bubble-top', *Daddy's Girl* was badly damaged by an American flak battery protecting the Remagen Bridge on 10 March 1945.

30

P-51D-5 44-11222/*Evelyn* of Lt Frank Rea Jr, 368th FS, East Wretham, March 1945

Rea bellied *Evelyn* in at East Wretham on 17 March 1945 after its main gear failed to extend. His replacement aircraft was elderly P-51B-15 42-106876, which, on 9 April 1945, he used to damage an Me 262. Four days later Rea was in the thick of the action again when he destroyed a locomotive and shared in the destruction of three others. He served with the 368th from January to September 1945.

31

P-51K-5 44-11685/*Janet* (left side), *Elva May* (right side) of Lt John D Cooley Jr, 368th FS, East Wretham, 1945

Cooley flew with the 368th from January to September 1945, destroying two locomotives and damaging a third with this fighter. *Janet* was eventually passed on to the USAAF's occupational forces post-war.

32

P-51D-10 44-14127/*DilBert* (left side), *Lil' Marge* (right side) of Lt Robert W McIntosh, 369th FS, East Wretham, March 1945

McIntosh served with the 369th from January to September 1945, and in that time his sole kill was a Soviet Yak-9, erroneously shot down on 18 March – he was flying P-51D-20 *Gloria Mac* (44-72435) at the time. This machine did enjoy a modicum of aerial success, however, for Lt James R Parsons Jr used it to down a Bf 109 on 11 September 1944.

33

P-51D-15 44-15015/ *"Babe"* of Lt Vernon T Judkins, 369th FS, East Wretham, 1945

Judkins flew with the 369th from August 1944 to September 1945. Despite failing to destroy any aircraft either in the air or on the ground, he did inflict damage on a locomotive, a truck and a marshalling yard on 11 February 1945 – the identity of the Mustang he flew on this occasion remains unknown.

34

P-51K-5 44-11574/*MARILYN BETH* (left side), *Miss Virginia* (right side) of Capt William F Stepp, 370th FS, East Wretham, 1945

Completing 57 mission (270 combat hours) between September 1944 and September 1945, Stepp destroyed one locomotive and killed four-five soldiers while strafing in another Mustang. Lt John F McAlevey was flying *MARILYN BETH* on 13 April 1945 when he shared in the destruction of eight locomotives and damaged three others.

35

P-51D-20 44-72425/*Gloria Mac* of Lt Robert E McCormack, 369th FS, East Wretham, March 1945

Joining the 369th FS in December 1944, Robert McCormack had completed 23 combat missions (123 hours) by VE-Day. He too got a Yak-9 (in this machine) on 18 March 1945, which proved to be his sole aerial kill. *Gloria Mac* was supplied to the Swedish Air Force post-war.

36

P-51D-10 44-14117/*Stinky* of Lt Joseph W Mejaski, 369th FS, East Wretham, March 1945

'Shoot everything that moves' Mejaski served with the 369th from June 1944 through to February 1945, completing 75 missions and 300 combat hours. On 11 September 1944 he destroyed two Ju 88s and damaged three others on the ground south of Merseberg while flying this P-51. *Stinky* was severely damaged in a crash-landing on 7 March 1945.

37

P-51D-15 44-15371/"*HAPPY*" of Capt James L Way Jr, 368th FS, East Wretham, March 1945

Serving with the 368th from January to September 1945, Way was assigned two Mustangs during his time in the ETO. "*HAPPY*" was the first of these, and he used it to share in the destruction of three locomotives. 44-15371 was lost on 19 March 1945 when Lt Clifton Enoch Jr inexplicably crashed and was killed while chasing an Me 262 near Halle, in Germany.

38

P-51D-15 44-15215/*TORCHY* of Flt Off Harley E Berndt, 369th FS, East Wretham, March 1945

Flt Off Harley E Berndt damaged a Yak-9 (in P-51D-15 44-15007) on 18 March 1945 in the one-sided clash between the 359th FG and the Soviet Air Force over eastern Germany. Berndt, who saw service with the USAF post-war, named all his fighters – ranging from the P-51 through to the F-106 – *TORCHY*. He served with the 369th from January to August 1945, then transferred out.

39

P-51D-20 44-72067/*OLE' GOAT* of Maj George A Doersch, 368th FS, East Wretham, April 1945

'Pop' Doersch flew two tours totalling 158 missions and 567 hours, his first spell in the ETO being with the 370th FS – he claimed ten of his 10.5 aerial kills with this unit. Doersch also strafed extensively, and shared in the destruction of 13 locomotives. *OLE' GOAT* was lost on 9 April 1945 when Doersch bellied the bomb-damaged fighter in near Frankfurt. He retired from the Air Force as a colonel in 1967 and went to work for the Hughes Aircraft Corporation, retiring in 1989. Doersch passed away on 1 December 1994.

40

P-51D-25 44-72746 of Lt Col Donald A Baccus, CO of the 359th FG, East Wretham, April 1945

Lt Col Donald Baccus became the 359th FG's final wartime CO on 7 April 1945, and he remained in command until 16 September. He was posted in from the 356th FG, where he had led the 359th FS from June 1943 until April 1944. Baccus then became Deputy CO of the 356th FG, and also

led the group for a short time in late 1944. He scored all five of his aerial victories with the 356th FG, 'making ace' on Christmas Day 1944. Baccus also claimed four ground kills, one of which he scored (in this very machine) with the 359th FG on 17 April 1945.

41

P-51D-15 44-14870/*PETER E. Jr.* of the 368th FS, East Wretham, April 1945

This machine was used by Capt Thomas J McGeever to destroy an Fw 190 parked on Gotha airfield on 21 November 1944.

42

P-51D-20 44-72208/*DELECTABLE* of Lt Emidio L 'Dago' Bellante, 370th FS, East Wretham, April 1945

Bellante joined the 370th in March 1945 and transferred out in July. His big day came on 13 April when he shared in the destruction of eight locomotives and damaged three more while flying this particular P-51. *DELECTABLE* was sold to the Swedish Air Force post-war.

43

P-51D-5 44-13893/*Caroline* of Capt Thomas P Smith, 370th FS, East Wretham, April 1945

Thomas Smith completed a truncated ETO tour in April 1945, having spent five months (April to September 1944) on the run in Occupied Europe after bailing out of his fuel-starved P-47 over the Netherlands on 11 April 1944. Eventually flying 76 missions, the highlight of Smith's tour came on 21 November 1944 when he shot down two Fw 190s and damaged two more whilst flying *Caroline*.

44

P-51D-20 44-72366/*HUBERT* of Lt Rene L Burtner, 369th FS, East Wretham, May 1945

Rene Burtner's *HUBERT* was used by Lt Fred McGehee to shoot down two Bf 109s on 24 March 1945. As for Burtner, his official claims consisted of three aircraft destroyed on the ground. However, on 18 March 1945 he also destroyed three Yak-9s – one of which he shot down – while flying this very machine. The stripes on 44-72366's dorsal strake denoted that Burtner was a flight leader. This aircraft was also sold to the Swedish Air Force post-war.

45

P-51D-25 44-73102/*SCREAMIN DEMON II* of Capt Andrew T Lemmens, 370th FS, East Wretham, 1945

Lemmens flew two tours, serving with both the 368th and 370th FSs, as well as the HQ Flight. In that time he completed 133 missions, totalling 524.5 hours, and scored three aerial kills. His first 'bubble-top' Mustang was P-51D-15 44-155521 *SCREAMIN' DEMON*, which was also coded CS-V. Ray Wetmore used 44-155521 to 'bag' his Me 163 on 15 March 1945, and it was eventually lost on 9 July 1945 when Lt George 'Turk' Turinsky bailed out over Norfolk after losing oil pressure during a routine training flight.

46

P-51D-15 44-15277/"*CisCo*" of the 370th FS, East Wretham, early Autumn 1945

Something of a mystery machine, this unusually decorated Mustang was one of the last P-51s assigned to the 359th

FG in its final weeks in the ETO. No combat reports revealing its wartime history have been located to date.

47

P-47D-6 42-74676/*Blondie II* of the 370th FS, East Wretham, Summer 1945

Unlike the 368th's P-51B two-seat 'hack', this P-47 was stripped of all its armament and the gunports faired over. Supplied to the group to give pilots experience of flying the Thunderbolt prior to the 359th potentially transferring to the Pacific theatre (where it would have flown P-47s), *Blondie II* was kept in immaculate condition during its brief time at East Wretham. This was no easy task for the groundcrews, as the weary fighter's radial engine leaked oil from myriad seals.

48

P-47D-2 42-8381 (War Weary)/*Little One* of the 3rd Gunnery and Tow-Target Flight, East Wretham, early 1945

Declared War Weary in late April 1944, this P-47 arrived at East Wretham from the 352nd FG, where it had been used by 13.333-kill ace Capt Donald S Bryan to claim his first 3.833 victories.

UNIT HERALDRY

1

359th Fighter Group

The group insignia was designed during December 1943 in a joint effort between the Group Intelligence Officers and Flt Lt R O N Lyne, who was the 359th's RAF Liaison Officer. The unicorn is the symbol of strength and virtue and the Latin phrase *CUM LEONE* means 'with lions', signifying the group's association with the RAF. At the top are three white stars, with three, five and nine points, placed on a midnight blue background. Finally, the red on the escutcheon represents the blood of courage, and is severed by a gold band of honour

2

368th Fighter Squadron

All three squadron emblems were designed by men from the unit in a contest which saw the three winners pocket five dollars apiece in prize money. The winning designs were chosen during April 1943, and officially approved on 6 July 1943. The single horn on each of the unicorns denoted that the units flew single-engined fighters. Each disc was painted in the squadron colour, with the 368th employing yellow. The 165th FS of the Kentucky ANG was the direct descendant of the 368th FS, and also used this emblem.

3

369th Fighter Squadron

The unicorn of the 369th FS is seen in full stride, portraying an aggressive attitude, on a red disc. The 167th FS of the West Virginia ANG inherited this emblem as the direct descendant of the 369th FS.

4

370th Fighter Squadron

The 370th FS badge showed the unicorn in a bucking posture, representing determination. The disc was dark blue.

COLOUR SECTION

1

Lt 'Tepee' Smith's P-51D-5 *Caroline* (44-13893), seen at East Wretham in April 1945 (*all colour photos from the T P Smith collection*)

2

Lt 'Tepee' Smith poses alongside *Caroline* (44-13893). The kill markings on the canopy frame represent the two Fw 190s that he shot down on 21 November 1944

3

A post-war line-up of 370th FS Mustangs. The nose on Thomas P Smith's *Caroline* has by now noticeably faded in comparison with the remaining three P-51s parked behind it. Second in line is Ray Wetmore's ex-ride 44-14733, now devoid of the scrolled name *Daddy's Girl*

4

The 370th FS's P-47D hack *Blondie II*, which was stripped of its armament and kept in immaculate condition

BIBLIOGRAPHY

Andrews, Paul M, Adams, William H and Woolnough, John, H *Bits & Pieces of the Mighty Eighth*

Army Air Force *Down to Earth - Fighter Attack on Ground Targets, To The Limit of Their Endurance, 359th Fighter Group 1943-1945*

Carter, Kit C and Mueller, Robert *The Army Air Forces in World War II Combat Chronology 1941-1945*

Cloe, John H *The Aleutian Warriors*

Ethell, Jeffery L *Komet the Messerschmitt 163*

Freeman, Roger A *The Mighty Eighth, The Mighty Eighth War Diary, The Mighty Eighth War Manual, Combat Profile - Mustang*

Miller, Kent *Jigger, Tinplate & Redcross*

Oliphint, John H *The Mad Rebel*

Rust, Kenn C and Hess, William N *The Slybird Group – The 353rd Fighter Group on Escort and Ground Attack Operations*

Scutts, Jerry *Lion in the Sky*

Späte, Wolfgang *Top Secret Bird – The Luftwaffe's Me 163 Comet*

Stafford, Gene B and Hess, William N *Aces of the Eighth*

INDEX

Figures in **bold** refer to illustrations, plates are shown as plate number(s) with caption locators in [brackets]